BABIES & BYLINES

Award-winning journalist Pallavi Aiyar has spent several years reporting from, and parenting in, China, Europe and Indonesia. She is the author of *Smoke and Mirrors*, *Chinese Whiskers* and *Punjabi Parmesan*. Pallavi is a World Economic Forum Young Global Leader, and a former Reuters fellow at Oxford University.

BABIES & BYLINES

PARENTING ON THE MOVE

PALLAVI AIYAR

HarperCollins *Publishers* India

First published in India in 2016 by
HarperCollins *Publishers* India

Building 10, Tower A, 4th Floor, DLF Cyber City, Phase II,
Gurugram Haryana – 122002, India
www.harpercollins.co.in

P-ISBN: 978-93-5177-560-7
E-ISBN: 978-93-5177-561-4

2 4 6 8 10 9 7 5 3 1

Typeset in 11.5/14.5 Lunux Libertine by
R. Ajith Kumar

Printed and bound at
MicroPrints India, New Delhi

For Ishaan and Nicolas

'And of all animals the boy is the most unmanageable, inasmuch as he has the fountain of reason in him not yet regulated; he is the most insidious, sharp-witted, and insubordinate of animals.'—Plato, *The Laws*

'You look like the rain, Mama, all black and golden!'—Ishaan at age three

'Can God defeat Darth Sidious?'—Nico at age four

CONTENTS

PROLOGUE

JANUARY 2001, LONDON

I was tipsy on wine and imagination. 'If it's a boy we'll name him Jenaro,' Julio pronounced and I sneezed up rivulets of Rioja in amusement.

'And if it's a girl?' I asked, wiping my mouth clean of its red stain, eyes fixed adoringly on this impossibly charming, erudite Spaniard, who had swept me off my feet these last few madcap months.

'Jenara,' he replied without a pause. 'Hopefully, it'll be twins and we can have a Jenara and Jenaro.'

I reached forward for a bite of alcachofas con jamon, swirling it carelessly in a bowl of olive oil. It felt ridiculously natural to be sitting in a Spanish restaurant, off Tottenham Court Road in London, imagining absurd names for our future children.

'We'll have to make sure they're not like these spoilt brats you see having meltdowns in supermarkets because their parents say no to candy,' I opined.

'Of course,' Julio nodded, adding, 'and they'll need to learn the value of money.' I agreed. Jenaro and Jenara would be polite, intelligent, polished, delightful at the dinner table and solicitous of those around them.

Julio and I eyed each other, perhaps a tad more clear-headedly than before. Something leapt in my stomach, and while it may have been the jamon, I think it was a fleeting, barely acknowledged, realization. Julio and I agreed on things. Important things. We matched, even if we were mixed.

I had just turned twenty-five, Julio was twenty-three. I was from India, he was Spanish. We had met as graduate students at the London School of Economics four months ago. He was figuring out a way to move to China that summer, where he was keen to live for the foreseeable future. I was off to Los Angeles to continue my master's degree in August.

This was obviously a silly conversation. Ours was obviously a silly relationship. Jenaro and Jenara were obviously nothing but vino-tinted ephemera.

1

THE PREGNANCY

2007–08, BEIJING

I stared at the double purple line emerging as fast as my heart was beating. A frigid wind blew in through the cracks in the window of the lone toilet of our hutong home, carrying with it the clickety clack of mah-jong pieces being shaken up for a new round. For a moment I felt like clambering on to the toilet seat, plastering my face against the window and waving the pregnancy test at the unsuspecting neighbours who gathered outside the corner store opposite our courtyard to play mah-jong every afternoon.

'*Wo huaiyun le*, I'm pregnant,' I'd shout out. But they probably wouldn't be able to hear me, and would chalk up my flattened face and wild eyes to one more drop in the ocean of inexplicable eccentricities foreigners were apt to display.

And so, instead, I held out the slender white wand with its stained purple lines, at the cats. 'Look!' I commanded them. Tofu and Caramel were in the toilet with me, huddled together to keep warm, and looking distinctly wary at my shenanigans. Caramel approached, somewhat reluctantly, and sniffed at the test, before snapping his head away in apparent disapproval.

I felt pretty much everything it was possible to feel: excited, anxious, confused, clear-headed, blabber-mouthed, tongue-tied. What I needed at that moment was a husband, to tell and hug and worry and celebrate with. But Julio was away in Brussels, sitting for one of a series of endless examinations required to enter the European Commission bureaucracy.

I pushed open the bathroom door, waded through ankle-deep snow in the courtyard and crossed over to the room opposite, which served as my office. I didn't know what to do with myself, or my news, so I just looked around, taking in the book-filled shelves we'd bought from Shaanxi province; the bright, stripy, Mexican rug that Caramel used to pee on copiously as a kitten; the fax machine so beloved of Chinese officialdom ('fax your request in triplicate' was the usual answer to any journalistic request for information), and my ageing laptop on which I had written my way to a career and sense of achievement.

Within the computer were folders with newspaper stories filed on-board the first train from Beijing to Tibet; written at the back of military aircraft en route to inspect Chinese military bases; from the Sunday cattle market of Kashgar in remote Xinjiang; and a whole book of reportage called *Smoke and Mirrors*. It was my first book, and the publication date was only four months away.

Life was good. It was stimulating, romantic and successful. When I'd first arrived in Beijing in 2002, with nothing but Julio's entreaties to support the decision, it had felt, at times, like I was on a fool's errand. I didn't speak the language, had no friends or family in the country to act as a safety net, and scant career prospects. A job as an English teacher at the Beijing Broadcasting Institute had secured me a visa, but that was the only security I had; a stamp on my passport that allowed me to live in Beijing.

Six years on, I was an award-winning China correspondent for one of India's top newspapers. My 'silly' relationship with

Julio had resulted in marriage in 2005. I had learnt to speak Mandarin. I lived in a modest, but nicely renovated, traditional courtyard house in the hutongs, the criss-crossing alleyways of imperial Beijing. I had mango-yellow living-room walls filled with photographs of holidays in Cappadocia and Luang Prabang.

But vacations were only an incidental part of life. Mostly, I was consumed by my job, which to me was an identity-defining and exhilarating adventure. I worked late into the nights on my manuscript after having run around the city interviewing dissidents, and scientists, for newspaper stories. I travelled at the drop of a hat, or rather, the ring of my mobile – to meet with heroin addicts in Yunnan province or Indian textile entrepreneurs in the wholesale markets of the Yangtze river delta.

A baby was going to unsettle this equilibrium. I knew this because for years I'd been listening to friends with kids smilingly repeat how 'children change your life'. I sucked in a lungful of cold air – the heating in our home had never worked well – and tried to restrain the emotional cartwheels the positive pregnancy test had set off.

I was really happy, yet it was a tempered happiness. I hadn't spent much time around kids. This was partly due to circumstances – my social circle consisted of people so young that the prospect of a family was as remote as Outer Mongolia, or those so old that their kids were away at university. At the time I hadn't known that the reason for this was that parents of young children don't 'do' social circles, being too wan, and rumpled, and just bone-tired to do much except sleep during the few hours their young ones permitted.

But, it was also by choice. Babies had never interested me. I'd never been struck by a longing to coo at a bundled-up newborn. I found toddlers having tantrums in airplanes intolerable. I was not a natural nurse. I found drool unpleasant. I disliked mess. I once caught sight of a friend tasting puréed baby food with her finger before feeding it to her seven-month-old. It had made me nauseous.

I recalled a scene from the year before, when a Norwegian friend of mine had come over for lunch with her four-month-old. It was the first time I was meeting her socially since the birth. We'd sat down for around two minutes before the red-faced mite had begun yowling and my friend immediately produced a breast at the dining table and began feeding him. I'd stared at my friend's face determinedly, willing myself not to look further down. It hadn't felt quite right to eat while the breastfeeding was going on, so I'd put down my fork and made small talk.

After what seemed like a geological epoch, the baby was placed on a blanket on the floor while we resumed eating. For around three minutes. My friend suddenly stopped mid-mouthful and began sniffing the air. 'Oh, no!' she'd exclaimed fondly. 'You've done poo poo.' A stinky diaper was then changed a few feet away from the dining table, following which the little one began to hiccup.

I finally offered for Auntie Li, our part-time maid, to carry the child around while we tried to continue eating. But the baby only wanted his mother and screamed blue murder when the maid tried to soothe him out in the courtyard.

Eventually, my friend had left within an hour of having arrived, her lunch mostly uneaten and various unidentified stains on her clothes. But what had really unnerved me were her parting words, frighteningly unlaced with irony. 'Thank you so much,' she'd beamed. 'This has been my nicest outing since the baby was born.'

Mine was a wanted pregnancy. I was thirty-two years old and had been in a relationship with Julio for almost eight years. It was time, I'd decided. In retrospect, however, I realize I hadn't decided, as much as responded – to my mother's queries; to what common sense concurred was 'normal'; to some kind of mysterious biological tick-tocking.

It was also a submission: to adulthood, to my commitment to Julio, to Darwin.

Julio and I had talked about kids off and on for years. It was light-hearted chit-chat. We'd assumed we'd have children, but never dwelt on details. I'd rarely paused to examine what I truly felt about motherhood, mostly because I feared that scrutinizing the subject might put me off it. And while I did not particularly want a baby, I also did not not want one.

Eventually, the scientific side of my temperament had taken over and I'd decided that a 'pilot project' was the best way forward. And so, in the summer of 2006, Julio and I acquired two kittens, the aforementioned Caramel and Tofu.

The cats required care, grooming and discipline. No longer could we just pack up our bags and leave for a vacation or work trip at short notice. We were responsible for their welfare and had to make provisions for them when away. No longer could we stay out late should the fancy take us. Someone needed to return home to feed the felines.

We took Caramel and Tofu to the vet and became familiar with vaccination routines and deworming pills. Tofu required supplemental vitamins, which we had to coax her into eating with every meal. We gave them baths and brushed out their tangled hair. We read up on ideal cat diets and fed them cooked liver and egg yolk. We bought cat-scratching posts and installed cat flaps to allow free access to the courtyard. We anthropomorphized them shamelessly, imagining how cute it would be if we could hold a cat birthday party to mark the first year of their adoption.

In short, Julio and I were transformed into doting cat parents. And despite the time and effort it required, we loved it. Doctor's visits, grooming, feeding – it could all be done enjoyably, I'd concluded. Of course a baby would require more of everything, but the general principles had been tried out and tested.

By mid-2007, I had completed the manuscript of my first book and been accepted to a three-month journalism fellowship at Oxford University. In the meantime, Julio had decided to sit the civil service exams for the European Commission. We were well on the path to adulthood.

On the eve of my departure for England we'd sat on the couch, looking out fondly at Caramel and Tofu as they gamboled about the pomegranate tree that shaded the courtyard. It would be a while before Julio and I would see each other, but once my fellowship was completed, we planned to meet up in Spain for the Christmas holidays. It was an unspoken assumption that we would begin to try for a baby then.

It had always amused me how talking about sex with anyone, except one's closest friends, was considered shocking, but chat about 'trying' for a child was the kind of thing you could safely discuss in detail with your elderly aunt's neighbour. Friends had told me that it could be a long-drawn-out process that took months, but that was just fine by us.

My Oxford stint over, Julio and I had a rather pleasant time holidaying in the shadow of the Alhambra in Granada and then on to the Great Mosque of Cordoba. A week later, however, Julio flew to Brussels for an exam, and I returned to Beijing to cover the visit of Indian Prime Minister Manmohan Singh to Beijing.

I'd barely had time to catch my breath with all the high-level politicking when I was off again, to the frozen hardscrabble of Hebei province, one of China's poorest regions. It was in the Hebei countryside that a young Indian doctor called Dwarkanath Kotnis had died in 1942, after spending four years in China, as part of a five-member medical team dispatched by leaders of the Indian National Congress to aid the Chinese in their war against Japan.

Dr Kotnis was only twenty-eight at the time of his arrival in China, having recently graduated from medical school. With slicked-back hair and a shy smile, the young doctor would go on to become the most enduring symbol of the warm Hindi–Chini Bhai Bhai sentiment that characterized Sino-Indian relations in the 1940s and '50s.

Kotnis was the only member of the medical team who never returned to India. He stayed on, fighting on the Chinese side, and eventually joined the Communist Party of China. In mid-1940, Kotnis was sent to work in Hebei. After arriving in Gegong village, he stayed on, treating the war-wounded until he died of an infection a few years later.

More than sixty years on, I found myself outfitted in an army-issue, padded overcoat, and layers of socks, tramping about Gegong village along with the twenty doctors from India and China who comprised the China–India Joint Medical Mission 2008. This was a public relations exercise undertaken by Beijing and New Delhi to commemorate the seventieth anniversary of the landing of the 1938 medical team from India.

The idea was that modern-day doctors from both countries would revisit areas associated with Kotnis's time in China and offer free medical consultations to the rural poor. They did this with the remarkable spirit of service that doctors working in poor countries often display. I, however, was cut of less noble cloth, and found it tedious and painfully cold after the first few hours. By the time we returned to the tiny hotel we were staying in, I didn't need much persuasion to knock back a few shots of baijiu, a vile grain-based liquor that tasted like nail varnish, but was undoubtedly warming.

'Well, you see it's like this,' a moon-faced doctor from one of Hebei's foremost medical missions had joked. 'Premier Zhou Enlai drank but did not smoke and he died at the age of seventy-eight. Chairman Mao, on the other hand, smoked but did not drink and he died at eighty-two. But Marshall Zhang Xue Liang, who both smoke and drank, lived till hundred!'

At that point our host, the vice mayor of Tangxian, the county Gegong village belonged to, had swung into action, leaving us with little doubt about his alcoholic alpha-male status, a much-coveted rank in provincial Chinese officialdom.

'You are all sissies,' he'd taunted the terrified Indian doctors, many of whom were teetotallers. 'You see, you have blood in your veins whereas I only have baijiu.' He'd proceeded to explain the 'correct' way to drink baijiu in China: 'First pick up your glass and place it to the lips. Next take a deep breath and suck in a small quantity while making bird-like noises – chirrup, chirrup. Never hide your glass with the palm of your hand. Be honest and open. Drain it in one go and then aaaah . . .' He'd held the glass upside down in triumph. 'Not even one drop of liquid should fall from the empty glass.' It hadn't.

By the time I'd returned to my room and lit up a sneaky cigarette, my head was reeling. I shivered as I took off the heavy coat and slipped under the duvet on the bed. It was then that my eye caught something glinting by the bedside lamp. With a start, I realized it was a strip of folic acid, something the Norwegian friend who had so enjoyed her non-lunch at my home had advised me to start taking once Julio and I embarked on the adventure of 'trying'.

I'd dutifully begun to ingest the pill, which Google informed me would help protect a fetus against spina bifida – a spinal defect. I had realized rather quickly that when people talked about how having children expanded your horizons, they should have specified the medical nature of these horizons. Within months, terms like hyperemesis gravidarum and placenta previa would trip off my tongue with the ease of a 'ni hao', or 'see ya later', or a 'wtf am I thinking?'

Spotting the folic acid between drags of my cigarette, I'd

realized that these smoky, boozy days were no longer tenable. Marshall Zhang Xue Liang may have lived to a hundred with all his booze and smokes, and without any folic acid tablets at all, but one imagined he'd never tried to conceive either.

I'd stubbed out the smoke and popped a pill, in the manner of a responsible adult. It was only when I was almost asleep that I'd hazily thought about how I hadn't got my period that month yet.

The episode with the pregnancy test took place around a week later. I was pregnant and it hadn't taken weeks or months or years, but a short break in Spain.

Julio eventually returned from his exam. When I told him, he held my hands and tears sprang to his eyes. The scene was straight out of a romance novel. We talked late into the night about our little girl, because I was sure, always had been sure, that I would have a daughter. She would be an astronaut, we decided, that is when she wasn't writing literary fiction. We considered names. We giggled. And we agreed to take a week's vacation in Cambodia to celebrate, during the upcoming annual Chinese new-year break.

The holiday hit all the right notes. We were enjoyably spooked by the deserted landscape of Kep, along the southern coast of the country, where the once grand mansions of the bourgeoisie lay wasting, unclaimed since the days of the Khmer Rouge. We ate fine food. I dashed off a travel piece for my newspaper. We swam, and exchanged languorous looks. I ostentatiously avoided wine.

It was only on our last day in the country, at a smart boutique hotel in the capital Phnom Penh, that I began to feel unwell. At first it was a slight queasiness, but by mid-afternoon I felt all sorts of stomach churnings. The constant taste of bile filled my throat. I felt too weak to stand up and too sick to lie down. Julio tried to distract me with offers of a swim, or dinner, or dessert. But the thought of swimming made me want to throw up. The thought of dinner made me want to throw up. And the thought of dessert made me want to throw up.

We had barely touched down in Beijing than I hurried to the hospital to see the first available doctor. She looked most solicitous as I described my symptoms, and we spent some time discussing what I'd eaten in Cambodia that might be causing this reaction. And then I mentioned the pregnancy. Her solicitousness was immediately replaced by an infuriating grin, a phenomenon I was to become most familiar with. Never could I have imagined that news of vomiting one's guts up day and night could elicit so many delighted smiles and coos of congratulations.

Me: 'I've never felt so sick in my life.'

Respondent: 'How wonderful! I'm so happy for you.'

The doctor sent me home with nothing but a few maternal clucks of sympathy and advice to stay hydrated. Taking anti-nausea medication when pregnant had not been proved to be safe. Of course it had not been proved to be unsafe either. But when it came to pregnancy a woman was stuck in a quagmire of less than scientifically robust advice, dare I say fetishes, about what she should be denying herself.

I was doubly denied, being caught between the traditional abstinences of Chinese culture and the curbs favoured by the latest fashion in Western 'science'.

The 'nos' piled up. 'No spice,' my Chinese doctor intoned. Unfortunately, Auntie Li, who often cooked for us, agreed, and so it came to pass that my Sichuan peppercorn-laced diet was suddenly replaced by endless small bowls of black chicken soup. The soup itself was insipid. But the black chicken it was made of resembled a particularly unattractive vampire bat, and watching parts of the butchered creature take up kitchen space did little to temper my 'morning', or rather my morning, noon and night sickness.

A pregnancy diet in China, it transpired, was no light matter.

The stentorian Auntie Li denied me foods that were too warming according to the ontologically exhaustive Chinese view of diet and health. Mangoes, peaches, coconut milk, pine nuts, lamb, coffee, chilli and so on were off the table. But guess what? Cooling foods had to be treated with caution as well. And so winter melons, cucumbers, sesame oil and another long list of digestibles were also treated with suspicion.

No booze, my Chinese friends proclaimed, and I will not forget the look I received from a waiter when I asked for a glass of white, to go along with my pumpkin soup (a warming food, to compound the faux pas), sometime during the eighth month of my pregnancy. He'd gasped and clutched at his throat as though he'd swallowed a fly.

I was also advised against getting massages, in particular foot massages, which was akin to requesting the vice mayor of Tangxian county to forgo his evening shot of baijiu. I loved writhing about in my seat as a masseur raked his knuckles across the arch of my feet or ruthlessly kneaded the metatarsals. I'd been a two-a-week foot massage girl for years. But now, masseurs across China spasmed away in alarm, upon spotting my swelling belly, violently shaking their dissent at my pleas for even a quickie.

The attendants at the gym I frequented became openly hostile as they realized I was planning to keep up my swimming routine through the pregnancy, until I was essentially ordered to stop visiting around the seventh month. In fact, the Chinese appeared to believe that no exercise was the safest option during a pregnancy. A woman with child was usually treated like an invalid, with solicitous strangers literally offering a shoulder of support were she to be found waddling about on the streets.

In August, a month before the baby was due, Julio and I braved the crowds to watch several of the sporting contests featured in the Beijing Olympic Games. As we approached the security queues at the match venues, dozens of eager volunteers were invariably galvanized into herding us into a 'special lane' billed as catering to 'The elder, the little, the sick, the disabled and the pregnant'.

But the Chinese were only the yin of restrictions, with Western prescriptions making up the yang. My Australian doctor, Dr Brooks, was much beloved of Beijing's expat community and he was laissez-faire, even encouraging, when it came to massage and exercise. But his list of 'nos' was nonetheless as long as the weeks of deprivation made nine months feel like.

Western science advised that a pregnant woman abstain from salad dressings like mayonnaise, raw vegetables in salads, sushi, cold cuts, and unpasteurized cheeses. I remember miserably passing on the Camembert, after having read an article titled 'Ten Foods Pregnant Women Should Avoid', which concluded thus: 'Feeding your baby what's best, beginning in utero, will help give your sweet pea the best start possible.' It proved impossible to look at salami without fear of listeria poisoning my sweet pea in utero after that.

Dr Brooks also informed me that drinking coffee in moderation was probably OK, and a very occasional glass of wine should be fine. What did 'probably' and 'should' mean, exactly? Was it also possible that coffee in moderation was not OK? Could a glass of wine turn out less than fine?

Economist Emily Oster wrote a book, *Expecting Better*, a few years after my pregnancy, about how risk aversion and the 'over interpretation of flawed studies' characterized obstetrics. Upon becoming pregnant and being ordered to desist from an array of foods and activities, she looked into the statistical data that served as the basis for all this advice and was shocked at how little was actually known. I was not an economist and did not delve into the statistics. But I was equally frustrated by the woolliness of much of the 'science'.

Abstaining from almost everything that was pleasurable appeared to be the safest, if not the most scientifically vigorous, route to protect your sweet pea. It took a hard woman indeed, or an economist, to resist such exhortations, when phrased like that.

And so I suffered, feeling besieged by teratogens from all sides: hot tubs, ibuprofen, microwaves, hair dyes and cats. Much as I'd like to act as if words like teratogen were part of my vocabulary because I was mega-literate, I had in fact never heard of the term until I began reading *What to Expect When You're Expecting*. This tome became my pregnancy bible, as it had been to the over ten million people the cover claimed had bought the text.

A 'teratogen', the book explained, was 'a substance that is potentially harmful to a developing embryo or foetus.' And by God, were these pesky things everywhere. The book broke down a nine-month-long pregnancy week by week and had sections on 'what you may be worried about' for every month.

The thing is that I was never worried about the issues it mentioned, until I read about them. For example, I had no idea that I might need to be concerned about an 'incompetent cervix' (I hadn't even known I had a cervix, leave alone whether it was competent) or that month three should have me asking questions about corpus luteum cyst. There were so many things that could go wrong and all in Latin: *abruptio placenta, placenta accreta, placenta previa.*

The worst was what the book revealed to me about the 'family cat'. Caramel and Tofu, it transpired, were not just the loveable, innocent pets of yore, but potential transmitters of the virus toxoplasmosis, an uber teratogen. Cats could pick up the pathogen by eating a bird or rat and it would then pass into their waste, which in turn could infect a pregnant woman and her sweet pea with horrible consequences.

I would have been sick with worry, if being literally sick all the time hadn't taken up all my capacity to be sick.

I had hyperemesis gravidarum, or an exaggerated form of morning sickness, which *What to Expect* said afflicted less than one in 200 pregnant women. There is no other way in which I would have liked less to be exceptional. Kate Middleton would suffer from the same, a few years down the line, but while the Duchess of Cambridge got to rest in hospital, I had to hold down a job as *The Hindu* newspaper's China correspondent.

The pregnancy-related norm I personally found to be the most ill-conceived was that of keeping it a secret for the first three months. The reasoning lies in the much higher chance of miscarriage in the first trimester, so that many don't consider a pregnancy to have really taken hold until the fourteenth week or so. But what is a working woman with hyperemesis gravidarum to do?

In retrospect I should have just told my employers and cut myself some slack. But, to begin with I wasn't even sure whether I was merely being weak and pathetic in my reaction to what everyone, including my doctor, assured me was 'normal'. Always that infuriating grin, followed by the jolly 'congratulations' as I tried desperately to explain that I couldn't even keep liquids down for long.

I felt unworthy and feeble. Was I being a hypochondriac? With Kate Middleton's celebrity hyperemesis gravidarum still in the future, no one seemed to really understand my condition.

I was also deeply worried about underperforming at work, because I was a committed feminist and a thorough professional. I took great pride in working extra hard on every story until it was as accurate, chiselled and evocative as possible. And my sense of ownership over my bylines was strong. To cut corners and churn out banalities would not only hurt my professional reputation, it would hurt *me* in the doing. Most of all, I genuinely didn't want to miss out on the action. Being on top of the China-related story du jour was intertwined with my sense of worth.

I knew I'd need a few months off after the baby was born (I'd calculated three would be enough), but the idea of taking leave, or even taking it easy, when the baby was nothing more than a seven or eight-week-old fetus, appeared absurd. It had certainly not been part of the plan.

And so I winged it. I was 'luckier' than many in that I operated far away from headquarters and only talked to my bosses over email. The annual meeting of the National People's Congress (NPC), China's parliament, rolled around. I crawled to the desk every morning and wrote about it. I made phone calls. I cried with exhaustion. I tried eating ginger, which is what everyone told me was the solution. And I took vitamin B6, another ostensible anti-emetic. I kept throwing up. It was debilitating

And then just as I was about to give up – on my job and my sanity – the nausea miraculously eased. By around fifteen weeks of the pregnancy, I began to be able to spend several hours without sticking my head in the toilet. I ate pasta and marvelled, as nothing happened. I noticed that the pomegranate tree in the courtyard seemed about to bear fruit.

It was also finally 'safe' to disclose the pregnancy and so I announced it to friends, family and the office. I experienced twinges of guilt when I wrote to my boss. It felt like a confession. Like what I was really announcing was that I would soon be entering into an arrangement in which I would be drawing a salary for 'free', courtesy my maternity leave. And I thought it wouldn't be too unreasonable for the newspaper to politely reply that since I now had other priorities, they would be relieving me of my duties.

They did no such thing. And yet, the guilt never wholly disappeared. These were self-imposed feelings at one level. But they also pointed to how far I had internalized the guilt structured into modern 'feminist' society, where men and women were notionally equal, so that a pregnancy felt like asking for the kind of special consideration that flew in the face of that equality.

Under present arrangements, it was understandable why an employer might prefer a male employee over a female of equal calibre. After all, chances were the latter was going to be overwhelmed by the demands of pregnancies and child rearing, with all the attendant physical and emotional distractions from the job that these entailed. Was it worth investing in a woman's career if she was only going to choose to stop working at full tilt, or even altogether, usually just when that investment had begun paying off?

These were age-old arguments against female equality in the workforce. It was why employers had traditionally paid women less. It was also why so many talented and dynamic women were forced into lives of domestic desperation. There was something rotten in this metaphysics of the workplace. It stank of misogyny. It was rancid with inequity, despite its protestations to the contrary.

I was increasingly convinced that the only way in which this conundrum of biological difference between the sexes could be overcome was by elevating fatherhood to the same hallowed footing as motherhood. Only by enforcing paternity leave – not offering it as an option, but by mandating it – would the guilt I had felt as a female professional on maternity-related leave, be assuaged.

Were employers to know that male and female employees would require a change of pace in their careers during their years parenting young children, merit, rather than gender, would be the genuine determining criteria for career advancement. Women might, for the first time, have a genuine choice about their goals, rather than the false consciousness that passes for choice today. And men would finally be given the social and economic sanction necessary to find fulfilment and value in their role as fathers.

My guilt pangs were, however, temporarily overcome, as the nausea passed and I entered the second trimester feeling chipper and raring to go. I travelled around India on a book tour as my China travelogue, *Smoke and Mirrors*, was published. Once back in China, I resumed reporting in earnest, flying to Shenzhen for a story on telecom giant Huawei.

What to Expect confirmed that month four of pregnancy marked the beginning of a three-month slot that 'for most women is the most comfortable'. Following this breezy introduction, however, it launched into a distinctly less sunny section on 'What you may be feeling', with bullet points listing: fatigue, constipation, heartburn, flatulence, nasal congestion, varicose veins on legs and/or haemorrhoids and bleeding gums.

Happily, I remained free of these afflictions and was shining with health as I arrived at the hospital for my twenty-week ultrasound. This was the scan that would reveal the gender of the baby. Julio held my hand, as the technician seemed to take an inordinate amount of time staring at the black-and-white blob on the screen that was our baby in the making. 'It's very active,' she remarked at one point, and indeed the blog appeared to be contorting non-stop.

Finally, she looked at us, and smiled. 'Congratulations, it's a boy.' It feels terrible to admit it now, but I felt like the air had been kicked out of me. What had happened to our lovely, feminist, literary astronaut? Boys were rough. They were hyper. They lacked fine motor skills. And they had penises. I didn't fancy facing one every time I had to change a diaper at all.

And then a second later, I was elated. The blob was a boy! I was weepy with the enormity of it. Julio and I exchanged proud, parental looks. We were going to have a literary astronaut feminist who happened to be male, that's all. But what would we name him?

Finding Western Indian hybrid names for girls was easy: Maya,

Tia, Tara, Anita, the choice was vast. But boys' names were less mutable. My mother suggested Dhananjay. We declined. In true imaginative European tradition, Julio's father (who also happened to be named Julio) suggested: Julio. We declined.

Over time, I managed to make some headway in getting Julio to agree to Ishaan. This was a name I had always found alluring and vaguely exotic. Unfortunately, in the manner in which generational popularity afflicts names, much of the rest of India seems to have felt the same way. By the time our Ishaan was born, it had become impossible to shift in an airplane seat without bumping into one. But an even bigger problem was agreeing on a Spanish middle name.

The matter was finally resolved a few weeks before the due date as Julio and I sat watching a tennis match at the Beijing Olympics. We'd been hurried past the line for the 'little, sick, disabled and pregnant' and I'd even cadged some seats in the disabled seating area. As Rafael Nadal strode on to the court, Julio and I exchanged a look of perfect complicity. Of course, the sweet pea was going to be named Ishaan Rafael. Why hadn't we thought about it before?

Perhaps because we'd been too preoccupied with the childbirth coaching classes we were attending, to prepare for the big event. These consisted of a six-session series of lectures (and to Julio's consternation, some demonstration as well) by a curly-haired, American midwife, who symbolized a third variant of pregnancy fetishization. I'd become au fait with the Chinese traditional and Western scientific approaches, but I was now about to be inducted into the American world of granola natural.

The midwife belonged firmly to the 'take back the birth' school – a grass-roots movement in the US deeply suspicious of medical interventions in the birthing process. This was a philosophy that at its bare basics could be summed up as: epidural pain relief = bad; au naturel home birth with baby delivered in bathtub = good;

C-section = very bad; moist-eyed husband cutting umbilical cord post-birth himself = very good.

Classes usually kicked off with a fifteen-minute birthing video in which we were subjected to gory close-ups of labouring moms panting, and infant heads crowning. Given that for the majority of us attending, our only prior relationship to labour came from having watched Hollywood movie scenes that started with 'Oh my God! My water has broken,' and then skipped to a crying infant being passed to a smiling mother, the experience was pretty intense.

The majority of our classmates were westerners and all were first-time parents. As the birthing videos progressed in graphic mucous-drenched detail, the husbands in the room tended to gently massage their spouses' bellies, or tenderly stroke their necks in comfort. The wives usually gripped their partners' hands tightly, giving them the occasional wan smile. All that is, except for one husband, mine, and one wife, me. In our case I had to massage Julio's back in reassuring comfort while he went as limp as a jellyfish with fear. 'There, there, it's not so bad,' I would murmur along with the other husbands.

In the event, Julio only managed to sit through one of the four birthing movies we watched, with his eyes open – the one that showed a C-section. That the mother in question wasn't screaming in pain as the baby was fished out helped. All in all the whole procedure looked far prettier than the different kinds of vaginal labour we had been subjected to in previous classes. I was beginning to understand the overwhelming preference for caesareans that urban Chinese women seemed to have. Some 40 per cent of women in Chinese cities voluntarily opted for C-sections over natural births.

Our instructor switched off the C-section video and turned around to face the class with a strained smile. 'Now, the most important thing to remember,' she said, with false cheer lacing her voice, 'is that even if you find yourself forced to have a caesarean, you must not think of yourself as a failure.'

Other bits of advice included staying at home for as much of the labour as possible, trying to visualize a calming scene on a beach in lieu of pharmaceutical pain relief, and regular perineum massage. I had to go back home and look up 'perineum' in my *What to Expect.* Like with the 'cervix', I hadn't known I had a perineum, and certainly not one that needed massaging.

At our last class, around three weeks before my due date, we took a break from birthing DVDs and instead the midwife showed a video featuring a wrinkled newborn squirming and bobbing about his naked mother's upper body, until he'd sniffed out a nipple to latch on to. This was our introduction to the 'baby-led latch', much beloved of modern lactation consultants (I was not only discovering parts of my body, but entire professions). This method focuses on allowing a baby to find her own way to her food source, naturally, without the outside 'interference' of the mother or a nurse.

Julio and I were both rather bored by the breastfeeding session. Childbirth was where all the action was, so to speak. I hadn't given breastfeeding much thought at all, except to have decided that I'd do it for a bit and then stop when I returned to work. How innocent I'd been. I'd had no premonition of the marital strife, sense of failure, strangers staring at my nipples, pain and guilt that the drama of breastfeeding would bring in its wake.

In fact, I had no idea of the storm that parenting an infant would break on to my until then unruffled and content life. Throughout the pregnancy I had assumed motherhood would be about me, and my decisions: when to return to work, when to breastfeed and when not to, what foods to deny my child, what standards of behaviour to demand. It simply hadn't occurred to me that motherhood would be as much about my baby, and that the baby might have its own ideas, personality, behaviour and needs, which could be contradictory to my own.

I remember chatting with Auntie Li about post-baby, domestic arrangements. I'd wanted her to start work for us full-time so that she could assist with the baby in addition to her housekeeping responsibilities. Since I worked from home, I'd assumed the little one would lie quietly in a bassinet by my feet, while I banged out stories on my laptop and Auntie Li cooked or cleaned. When it was time for me to go out to conduct an interview, Auntie Li could exit the kitchen and take charge of the infant.

Auntie Li had cleared her throat and broken the news as kindly as possible. 'You don't have much experience with babies,' she'd said. 'You'll need a full-time nanny if you're going to work.'

'Oh?' I'd thought to myself, not totally convinced but willing to go along. I'd hired Auntie Li's sister-in-law, Auntie Mei, as a nanny-in-waiting. As further preparation, Julio and I bid a tearful farewell to our lovely courtyard home in the hutongs, and moved into a more sanitized, temperature-controlled, apartment in the diplomatic compound.

Everything was in readiness by the time my due date approached. My mother had arrived from Delhi and was installed in the guest room. I had a birth plan printed out in accordance with the advice from my childbirth preparation classes. Julio and I had picked out an antique bassinet from southern China. We'd bought burp cloths and swaddling blankets. A friend, who'd given birth a few months earlier, had handed me an inflatable tube to sit on (in case of a sore perineum) and some nipple cream. All that was left to do was to wait.

My due date arrived. I woke early, at 5 a.m., with a full bladder, an annoyingly regular occurrence in the third trimester. I sat down on the toilet, looked down bleary-eyed, and blinked. My heart raced. It was happening. Bang on time.

'Bloody show,' I yelled, waddling out into the bedroom where a sleeping Julio lay. 'Bloody show,' I repeated in excitement, knocking on the door to my mother's bedroom. They awoke to look at me blankly, as though beholding a cursing lunatic. I was irritated by the reaction. Yes, I probably looked a tad deranged with my enormous belly wobbling about inside my rumpled pyjamas, but it was clear neither my husband nor mother had been reading their *What to Expect.*

A lot less gentle sounding than the movie staple of 'water breaking', a 'bloody show' was another common sign of the imminent onset of labour. The mechanics behind the 'show' were as unlovely as the rest of Ob–Gyn plumbing. The cervix dilated to rupture capillaries and cause some bleeding, which usually meant that labour would start within twenty-four hours.

I spent the day in a state of frenzied anticipation, pacing up and down the house, attuned to every twinge and cramp in my belly. By dinner time the twangs began to become somewhat intense. By midnight I was gasping and letting out little yelps, but my midwife instructor's words about staying put at home for as long as one could bear it, had made an impression. I imagined childbirth to be so painful that 'giving in' at this stage frightened me about my ability to withstand what was to come. And so I groaned and puffed away in my bedroom, while, much to my chagrin, Julio slept through the noise.

In the days to come, when I brought up this sloth in the face of my labour, Julio always justified his somnolence by alluding to still more of the midwife's infernal advice. It's true, she had mentioned that the best thing a husband could do while his wife laboured in the early stages at home was to get some sleep, so that he'd be fresh for the hours ahead in hospital. However, considering how Julio hadn't taken on board too much of what happened at the childbirth preparation classes, in fact refusing to open his eyes during the majority of the videos, it was strange how he seemed to have taken this particular instruction so much to heart.

By 2 a.m. I was in an agony of contractions. Outside, heavy sheets of rain began to shift across a lightning-splintered sky. Caramel and Tofu stared up at me, their pupils dilated and shining in their glassy, green eyes. I shook Julio and my mother into wakefulness. Even the midwife would have agreed that it was time to head to the hospital.

2

THE BABY

SEPTEMBER–DECEMBER 2008, BEIJING

Eight hours later, I lay sweat-soaked and contracting on a hospital bed. I'd taken all the midwife's advice. I'd spent an hour soaking in the maternity ward's jacuzzi, bounced up and down on a birthing ball, taken regular sips of water, imagined lying on the beach, and put on Mozart. But finally, I'd reached my limits. I was 'almost there' according to the nurse, but I didn't care. I. Wanted. Drugs. IMMEDIATELY.

The pain of the contractions was like a roar in the ears by now, but nonetheless, I heard the anaesthesiologist quite clearly as he struggled to poke me in the spine with a needle. 'Damn, it's not going in,' he muttered in Chinese. 'I understand Mandarin, you git,' I wanted to yell at him, but was too terrified of everything: the pain, the epidural, the baby that was trying to batter his way out of my body. It felt demonic. I clutched Julio's hands and screamed into the antiseptic horror of the birthing room. And then like a switch being flicked, the anaesthesia kicked in, and I promptly fell asleep.

I woke to the sight of an ageing Australian peering at my nether regions. 'Time to push,' Dr Brooks announced cheerfully, as I blinked vacantly. I was basically numb from the waist down, and disoriented from the waist above. But, with overdone encouragement from all the people in the room – Julio, my mother, the nurse and Dr Brooks himself – I began 'pushing'. Since I couldn't feel anything at all, this was more of an imaginative exercise than a physical one.

It felt like we were all under water, as I watched my mother's lipsticked mouth open and close around the words, 'Come on, Pali!' – the sound distorted and delayed. To add to the surrealism, Dr Brooks kept urging me to assume an 'Indian bum' position. At first I thought I was hallucinating, a reasonable supposition given that by that point I'd been in labour for as far back as I could remember. But then it dawned on me that he was referring to the Indian propensity to squat on toilets. Didn't he realize how inappropriate this instruction was, given whom he was instructing?

Before I could muster a protest, Dr Brooks suddenly unsheathed what looked suspiciously like a bathroom plunger. He indicated the clock. It had been an hour since pushing had commenced, to little effect. 'We're going in,' he announced happily, and in he went.

A few moments later, I felt my body pop and empty; like a balloon that a careless toddler had abruptly stepped on. 'He's not a whopper,' Dr Brooks commented chattily, as Ishaan was weighed, and then placed on my chest. I choked on emotion so visceral that it packed a physical punch. Everything was bloody, but also beautiful. Ishaan writhed, his bony body still coated with my insides. Julio stepped up to cut the umbilical cord with unexpected felicity. I felt like a magic veil had lifted to allow me to behold the raw truth of existence: harsh and horrific; tender and wondrous.

Ishaan's face was purple and wrinkled, with the old-new look of the just born. Toothless, hairless, creased and shiny, his eyes were wide open and alert. 'Oh,' gasped my mother in rapture. 'He looks so peaceful and wise. Just like the Buddha.'

It was 3 a.m. as I grimly shook the rattle, limp-wristed with exhaustion. Meanwhile, the red-faced monster I clutched with my other arm showed scant signs of any tiring as he screamed into the night, with facial contortions that rivalled Edvard Munch's darkest depictions.

'Shhh,' I murmured as soothingly as I could manage. But inside my head I wept with exhaustion and terror at what had happened to my life. The peaceful little 'Buddha' of a month ago had abruptly morphed into a writhing Damien who slept in half-hour increments, interspersed with hours of full-throated yowling.

Conventional wisdom about gentle rocking, checking for wet diapers and ensuring a full stomach seemed about as useful as offering a cup of chamomile tea to a raging bull. Ishaan could be as well fed and watered as the Indian president's favourite rose in the Mughal Gardens, as dry as the state of Gujarat, and as rocked as a passenger in the general compartment of an overnight train, and still be screeching his lungs out.

It began when he was around three weeks old. Until then he'd remained relatively peaceful, staring with equanimity at the visitors who showered him with stuffed toys. He'd slept for much of the day, although he had a tendency to wake up for long stretches at night, hiccupping.

The first evening he started screaming I thought my world had imploded. He pulled his little legs up to his chest, and went purple in the face, screeching non-stop for three hours or so. It appeared there was nothing I could do to help him and I was devastated. I shushed and rocked and fed and sang and then did it all over again, to no avail. Every scream was like a personal rebuke to my mothering skills. Each cry was asking for the help that I was unable to give.

And so began a daily ritual of hours of inconsolable crying, which tended to reach a crescendo at night. The doctors I spoke to – and there was a succession of them – casually diagnosed 'colic' and sent me home with gripe water, a sympathetic hand on the shoulder, and advice to get some sleep. What were these people smoking? I wondered. Did they really think a 'prescription' to get some shut eye would mean I'd actually be able to do so?

'Sleep when your baby sleeps,' was the standard soft-focus counsel given to new mothers, usually accompanied by pictures of a sweetly sleeping babe nestled against a dewy-skinned, adoring mother's cheek. But since my baby slept in short bursts, and at the oddest times, I was in a permanent state of jet lag. No matter how exhausted I got, I found it hard to unwind enough to relax into sleep, terrified by how brief any rest would be.

And it was not as if I was waking up to merely feed the baby back into gentle slumber, as was the norm for many mothers of newborns. I usually woke to full alertness, like an anti-terrorist squad at the news of a bombing. It often took hours of rocking and feeding and dancing and rattling to wrestle Ishaan back for another quick lie-down. He cried loudly through much of this, each yell a knife turning in my heart. There was nothing soft-focused, or gentle, or dewy about colic. It was raging and murderous and loud.

None of the doctors I consulted had convincingly been able to explain to me what exactly colic was. Since I wasn't getting any sleep, I used the fleeting moments of calm in the house when Ishaan was taking a rare nap, to research this strange affliction on the Internet. I'd always vaguely associated the term with stomach pains, particularly of the equine variety, having read *Black Beauty* as a girl. But why was my baby's tummy hurting?

The upshot of my extensive readings was that it was impossible to know. 'Colic' is a description rather than a diagnosis. It refers to an infant who cries more than three hours a day, for more than three days a week, for at least three weeks, and whose cries do not respond to standard parental interventions. It usually begins at around two to three weeks of age (spot on for Ishaan) and disappears by the fourth month. In other words, 'colic' in infants is just medical jargon for lots of crying.

There is no consensus on what causes this colicky crying, although plenty of folks, medically qualified and otherwise, have hypotheses ranging from lactose intolerance and acid reflux, to a fussy temperament and even parents passing off their own stress to their infants.

My mother, who was back in India by this time, consulted our well-regarded neighbourhood paediatrician in Delhi about Ishaan's sleeplessness. The doctor's response was the kind of drivel that drove me quite batty.

'Darling Pali,' my mum's email read. 'The doctor says it sounds like stress. She says *you* need to have no tension, because the baby picks up anything you may feel, or think. She says to hold him next to your heart and talk softly to him, telling him that no situation can change the love you have for him. Put on soft music that you like.' In other words, chamomile tea to a raging bull.

Did it never occur to these undoubtedly well-intentioned people that maybe I was stressed because of the baby, rather than being the cause of the baby's stress. Being told that I, or my 'stress', was the reason for Ishaan's unhappiness felt like one more item on an already interminable laundry list of pregnancy and baby-related issues that were the mother's 'fault'.

But nothing was more in the firing line of expectations and culpability than my breasts. Bloody breasts! How I'd come to hate them.

It had become clear very quickly after Ishaan was born that the days when my mammaries were my private business were over. This was unceremoniously driven home when two days post-partum, Dr Brooks, the Australian gynaecologist with a folksy turn of phrase, strode into the hospital room where I lay supine and, without so much as an if you please, copped a feel of my breasts. 'Good! Nice and firm,' he said approvingly, 'the milk's coming along well.'

Except it wasn't. I watched in misery as women around me pumped bottles full of milk, while all the squeezing of the world produced nothing but sore nipples from mine.

Our childbirth preparation specialist had warned that it might take a few days for a new mother's milk to come in and that in the while all a baby needed to be sated was teaspoon quantities of the colourless liquid called colostrum. Through the fug of my post-labour exhaustion I remembered the midwife's warnings about the cavalier attitude towards formula milk in Chinese hospitals. 'Resist all efforts to give your baby formula,' she had declared ringingly.

I'd paid only peripheral attention since I'd already made up my mind to exclusively breastfeed for a few months. Who wouldn't? After all, the health benefits of breastfeeding were the sacred truth of our times. There was rare scientific consensus on the fact that mother's milk made children smarter and healthier and better. Only the ignorant or extremely selfish didn't feed their babies. At worst I'd anticipated that feeding might be a tad boring, but I'd imagined it would also be sweet and heart-warming to watch your little one sip from the maternal cup.

And so my antennae were raised when the hospital nurses repeatedly insisted that the baby was hungry, which made him fussy. 'No formula,' I roared at them and stuck the babe to my boob for what felt like the trillionth time in the day. Ishaan sucked and sucked and I convulsed in agony. Not only did my nipples begin to bleed under his forceful clamping but my abdomen cramped in intense pain.

I pulled out my dog-eared copy of *What to Expect*, and began to read, for the first time, the section on post-partum care, accurately titled, 'Last but not Least'. I suppose it is natural for first-time mothers to focus on their pregnancy, but in retrospect it is ludicrous how I had envisaged labour to be a finishing line. It is, of course, only the beginning of a lifelong post-partum marathon. And yet, until that moment, I had hardly bothered to even skim read literature about what goes on once the baby is born.

What goes on is in fact rarely discussed publicly. Society acknowledges that labour is painful, but the pay-off is supposed to be that gorgeous bundle in your arms who makes all memories of the torment of the birthing process waft away aboard clouds of contentment. The reason for this silence on the post-partum, I concluded, was evolutionary. Who the hell in their right minds would volunteer to have kids if they really knew what was in store?

My *What to Expect* was brutally didactic. The cramps I was experiencing while nursing, it explained, were 'afterpains'. It turned out that labour contractions *did not end* with labour. Apparently your uterus keeps contracting after birth, the pains made worse by nursing, 'when contraction-stimulating oxytocin is released'. The two-paragraph-long by-the-by that the book devoted to this horrifying revelation breezily concluded, 'By the end of six weeks, you probably won't feel anything at all.'

There was more misery contained within the post-partum section – pain in the perineal area, bruises on the chest, incontinence, constipation, bleeding, depression and, oh yes, sore nipples – than pestilence in the middle ages.

The book cheerfully admitted, 'Tender nipples can make nursing a miserable – and frustrating – experience.' This was true.

'Most women,' it continued, 'fortunately, don't suffer for long.' The exceptions it seemed were those with 'barracuda babies' whose 'vigorous suck' meant that the 'soreness and cracking might become so painful' that the moms concerned 'may come to dread each feeding'. I wasn't going to argue with that either.

I devoured the longish section on breastfeeding techniques, becoming an expert on different nursing holds. The advice was listed like the Ten Commandments, full of 'thou shalts' and 'thou shalt nots'.

'Don't stuff the nipple into an unwilling mouth; let your baby take the initiative.'

'Nurse on demand, for as long as the baby wants. But be sure to get in at least eight-twelve feedings a day.'

'Make sure your baby's appetite is not sabotaged between feedings.'

This last injunction echoed my midwife's advice on preventing the baby from being fed any formula or water by nurses while we were still at the hospital. I would get nauseatingly familiar with the theory behind this diktat, according to which the female body *always* generates enough milk to feed a child. But it needs the stimulation of suckling to generate this milk. If a baby is offered formula, it misses a feeding on the breast, which means that less milk is produced, which in turn means the baby will require more formula, and the mom will produce less milk, locking mother and child into a vicious cycle that will end in breastfeeding failure and all-round misery. There is, lest it not be clear yet, no such thing as a mother with too little milk.[1]

And yet, every woman I met in those first few days after giving birth asked me precisely whether I had 'enough' milk – from aunts in New Delhi calling to congratulate us, to Auntie Li, our cook, and her sister-in-law Auntie Mei, our nanny-in-waiting. Nurses stared at my breasts with furrowed brows, as I sat with a suction cup attached to a breast, pumping away to try and extract something to prove once and for all that I did indeed have enough milk. But even five days post-partum, I was barely able to produce a tiny 10 ml of this maternal manna, despite having suffered the indignity of being mechanically milked for over half an hour. The instructions that came along with the hospital-supplied breast pump cheerily stated that 'most women' filled 100–110 ml bottles within 10–15 minutes of pumping.

'No good,' muttered a nurse with the physique of a Mongolian weightlifter, as she casually shook my 10-ml-filled bottle like a rag doll. 'No milk.'

Through all of this I persisted in repeating to my sceptical audience that I definitely had enough milk. I authoritatively explained to them that in fact there was no such thing as too little milk. They stared at me blankly. Undeterred, I continued my pedagogic endeavour, by waving my *What to Expect* in their direction. Every woman produced sufficient milk to feed her baby. It said so, right here.

Yet, with every repetition, I believed it less. My nipples were bleeding, my uterus in an agony of cramps, and my body worn out from the labour and the constant wakings to feed a baby who never seemed satisfied by what he was getting from the breast.

I tried to follow instructions about letting the baby nurse for as long as he wanted, but Ishaan could keep up his barracuda-style sucking for over an hour and still seem hungry, crying when I plucked him off. I had begun to dread the moment a nurse handed him to me. I wanted my breasts to go back to their usually reclusive state. I wanted my body to feel my own, rather than at the constant disposal of a baby who did nothing but cause me physical pain and fatigue.

I wanted to radiate happiness as I reclined on a hospital bed surrounded by flowers and smiling visitors who were secretly envious of my perfect life as they passed the warmly bundled, full-bellied baby around. I was used to being successful and admired. I was used to getting what I wanted: a first at Oxford, a handsome and loving husband, a career that gave me a public voice, and two beautifully groomed cats. I was willing to work hard, to be disciplined, and to use common sense: a combination of virtues that had served me well.

But for the first time, I was finding that hard work, and research, and good intentions were not producing their usual salubrious results. I was doing everything by the book, and yet I felt miserable and violated. I wondered if I was experiencing the famous 'baby blues'. I read that up to 80 per cent of new moms experience mild post-partum depression. But the label irked me. Depression implied an abnormal emotional state. But if what I was experiencing was anything to go by, it was a happy mom who was emotionally aberrant.

In hindsight, those first few days after Ishaan's birth were the prologue to one of the most important life lessons that becoming a parent drives home, year after year, phase after phase: there is much beyond your control; accept it. A mother, or father, can only try their best to establish patterns, but they cannot control their non-programmable flesh-and-blood children like a video game. They cannot prescribe when another human being will sleep or eat. They can work with their children's personalities, but they cannot create them.

'If you can't change a situation, change your attitude to it,' is one of the most frequently mouthed chicken-soup-for-the-soul-like platitudes. I had to become a parent before I realized just how profound, albeit confoundingly hard to implement, this syrupy adage is. But it took me years of metaphorically butting heads with my children before I grasped this, and I've never managed to actually put it into practice.

Regardless, becoming a mother is an undoubtedly valuable exercise in humility, although at the time it merely felt like one in humiliation. I remember thinking it wasn't very smart from an evolutionary perspective to kick a mom with bitten nipples and sleepless nights, when she was already down, following nine months of pregnancy and hours of wracking labour. God is a renowned sexist, but I felt pretty murderous towards science as well, for this nasty bit of biological misogyny.

On our last scheduled day in the hospital, the paediatrician, a young earnest-faced woman, walked in with Ishaan's charts and a worried look. The baby's weight had dropped since his birth, which while normal for a day or two, should have picked up by now. And he had a mild case of jaundice, requiring him to be placed under bright lights for a twenty-four-hour period, which would cause further dehydration. 'Let him have a bottle of formula,' she urged. 'Just one. Just for today. It won't affect your breastfeeding.'

It sounded like a medical prescription. But all the parenting experts I had been reading had warned against this moment of weakness. I felt a moment of lactation aporia, and see-sawed wildly between the options. And then my mother spoke up.

'Oh! Give him a "top feed", Pali,' she said, exhaling with barely concealed frustration at my obduracy. 'It's not a big deal. You always had one.' I looked at my most beloved progenitor in surprise, and it occurred to me to ask about her experience with breastfeeding when she was a new mom. I was horrified to learn that she'd fed me, supplemented with formula, for barely a month before 'returning to work', a euphemism for switching to the bottle. 'It's OK,' she said soothingly at my horrified expression. 'I didn't have enough milk, and that's what formula exists for.'

I was conflicted. On the one hand this revelation seemed terribly irresponsible. After all, there was no such thing as a mother who produced too little milk. And what was with the 'that's what formula exists for'? How inane! One might as well urge a pre-diabetic to gorge on chocolate cakes, because after all, 'that's what insulin is for'.

I come from a culture where we do not blame our parents for the ills of our lives. It had never occurred to me to be anything but grateful to my mother for bringing me up with much love and care. Yet, for the first time, I felt really let down by her. Hadn't she known the damage she could have caused me by failing to breastfeed? I thought back to the endless colds and coughs I'd suffered as a child. Would these have been alleviated by a few more months on the breast?

It transpired she hadn't known much at all. Over the next few weeks I discovered that my mom's standard responses to baby-related queries, or comments, ranged from 'Really? How was I supposed to know that?' to 'I don't know. It was thirty-seven years ago.'

But it struck me that had she even wanted to know, her ability to access information would have been sharply circumscribed without the Internet. I tried conjuring up a world without the endless rash of baby-related posts on my Facebook feed, without the twittering of parenting gurus, and without the constant 'suggestions' made by Amazon about the latest baby manual I might like to read.

For women of my mother's generation, ignorance must have functioned as a most effective anti-anxiety salve. How wonderful, from the mom's, if not always the baby's, point of view, to be able to turn your little one over on her tummy for a nap without a care for SIDS (sudden infant death syndrome). Or to take a baby for a car ride holding her peaceably in the lap, rather than having to force her flailing body into a car seat. Formula feedings, pacifiers, lax baby-proofing of the house, and early weaning (as opposed to the six months of exclusive breastfeeding that is the norm now) are common enough practices even today.

But the difference between the generations lies in the glorious lack of self-reproach that our mothers must have felt given their information-lean world. So much of the pervasive guilt-lacerating moms today has been manufactured by the ever-expanding corpus of contemporary 'baby science' and compounded by its near-ubiquitous availability.

In the months and years that followed, however, I came to realize I was wrong. Our mothers, as theirs before them, must have found inventively personalized ways and reasons to torture themselves. For anxiety, conflict and guilt are woven into the fabric of motherhood. The tempering influence of ignorance is merely relative. I can only imagine the new 'facts' our children will have to suffer when it is their turn at parenting. What if broccoli turns out to be carcinogenic? How angry will Ishaan be with me when he learns that I'd proudly fed him puréed cruciferous vegetables for months?

Back at the hospital, once the initial shock of having discovered my own under-optimal infant diet wore off, I began to look at the matter with barely acknowledged relief. I'd turned out OK. My brain hadn't calcified and my health was fair. Sure, I'd coughed a lot as a kid, but who was to say I would have been less phlegmy on a diet of breastmilk? My friends' breastfed offspring were as stuffy-nosed as the rest.

My mother's revelation was like the serpent in the Garden of Eden, holding out the delicious temptation of a few hours of unchewed nipples, unreproached breasts and a demonstrably well-fed baby. My own mother was giving me permission to do what it was taking every ounce of willpower not to cave in to. And so I nodded a weak assent to the doctor, and Ishaan was immediately fed a bottle, which he greedily sucked at until he looked full and fat.

For the first time since I'd begun labouring, my body felt like it had been cut some slack. The next two weeks passed in an emotionally fulfilling haze. We returned home to a non-stop stream of stuffed-toy-bearing visitors. Auntie Mei watched over little Ishaan like a hawk all day, even when he was napping, sitting on a stool next to his bassinet, her eyes taking in every twitch and tremble of his resting muscles. My mother adoringly reiterated her conviction of the baby's Buddha-like nature. I breastfed every few hours and topped up with some formula afterwards. I held Ishaan close to me and inhaled his powder-fresh baby smell.

I was still not fully healed from the damage caused by the vacuum extractor that Dr Brooks had used to suck Ishaan out of me and needed a cushion to sit down on. But slowly I began to feel stronger. The afterpains had almost vanished and breastfeeding was less painful than it had been at first.

And then, like an apocalyptic thunderstorm, Ishaan began his all-night screaming fits. We went free-falling into the void of colic. The spotlight was once again on my breasts and what was coming out of them. Every time we went to see a paediatrician about Ishaan's crying, the discussion would turn to breastfeeding. Admitting to topping up with formula made me shifty-eyed and panicky.

I knew, with a sinking heart, that I was a bad mother for having failed to exclusively breastfeed, possibly causing the colic that was making him (and us) so distressed. But the thought of round-the-clock feedings on the breast, interspersed with hopeless pumping of bottles of nothing, against the background of family and helpers endlessly chanting that the baby was hungry, was suffocating and denuding.

We switched to a hypo-allergic formula. There was little improvement. Plenty of breastfed babies suffered from colic too, so the connection with formula was tenuous. And Ishaan's diet was 'mixed', consisting of both breastmilk and formula, which made any causal relationship even more problematic to establish. Nonetheless, I was tortured by the possibility that the colic was entirely my fault, for having given in to that first bottle of doctor-recommended artificial milk at the hospital.

Where was Julio, my most beloved husband and companion, in the midst of all the kerfuffle? Although the European Union only mandated a few days' paternal leave, Julio had taken a full month off, using up his annual vacation, in order to fully participate in the magical and important first month of our new baby's life. At least that had been the thinking. That raising a child would be a fifty-fifty joint venture was an assumption I'd never even felt the need to articulate. It had been the common-sense notion at the base of my exemplarily equal relationship with Julio.

People like Julio and me – young, hyper-educated and cosmopolitan – were unselfconsciously post-feminist. We had never felt the need to address traditional gender divisions because they'd never existed in any tangible way in our relationship. Julio cooked because I'd never learnt to. I travelled more for my job than he did. We supported each other's career moves. We'd never conceived of the need for a joint bank account. I'd kept my last name after we married.

And yet, now that the baby was here, it was not Julio who was suffering bleeding nipples and perineal tears. It was not Julio who was tormented by feelings of culpability and failure. Even through the screaming he read newspapers, and had hot showers, and thought non-baby thoughts. Yes, he rocked Ishaan and put him to sleep on occasion. Yes, he changed some diapers and he tickled the baby under the chin during a rare moment of calm.

But mostly he read. Later, I was to discover that he'd also started writing a novel during his month off from work, and played the stock market (to no good effect). This was incomprehensible to me. Julio was just getting on with his life, which now happened to include a cranky baby. There was, however, no getting on with my life. I couldn't even locate my life on a map if asked to.

In the days and weeks after Ishaan was born, the world economy almost collapsed and Lehman Brothers did. China conducted its first successful spacewalk. Sarah Palin paraded around in $150,000 worth of designer clothes, and Barack Obama became the first African-American president of the United States. I was a professional news hound and I did not care. I *could* not care. I could barely use the toilet without interruption.

Julio was defensive when I accused him of not doing enough. 'I've taken a month's leave,' he said. It was true. He had. And it is also true he could not have given birth to the baby or breastfed him. 'I'm not a mother,' Julio said. And there it was. Wham! The first hint of a gendered discourse entering our till now unstratified relationship.

I didn't admit it to myself at the time, but while I'd obviously known that Julio could not breastfeed, what I'd really wanted was for him to feel as tired and discouraged and overwhelmed by it all as I did. There is patently a biological asymmetry in infant rearing. But that didn't prevent me from desiring an emotional and mental equality, the lack of which seemed far more egregious.

I resented Julio for having the mental space for adult pleasures like reading and politics. When he complained of being tired because he'd 'only' had six hours of (continuous) sleep, I felt murderous. I wanted him to be as engrossed in the infinite minutiae of babydom as I was forced to be. I didn't want to be alone on this frightening and tedious journey.

Biology had already twisted our once symmetrical marital partnership into a lopsided arena, heavily weighted on the female side. But what was the cause of this difference in the impact that the baby seemed to have on our brain (mine was occupied, Julio's only partially visited), and hearts (mine was overwrought, Julio's was not), and muscles (mine were coiled tense, Julio's were just weary on their reduced six hours of sleep)? Was it nature or nurture? Therein, it seemed to me, lay a key conundrum for gender relations, feminism, public policy and parenting.

Biological equality was impossible, everyone agreed. The sharing of housework – cooking, cleaning and the physical aspects of childcare, like putting a baby to bed – was possible, everyone agreed. But when it came to the prospects of equivalence in the less tangible, psychological responses to parenthood, the picture was muddier.

The gulf that opened up between Julio and me in that first month of colic only grew wider with the years. This gulf was often guilt-shaped. I felt guilty as soon as any work-related opportunity threatened to take me away from Ishaan. My email inbox would announce that I'd been honoured with some fellowship or the other, and the person who'd react with unreserved excitement would be Julio. My own first response was always interlaced with guilt over extra 'honour'-related time commitments, or travels that hadn't even been discussed yet.

The gulf had many avatars. There was the inability-to-compartmentalize-work-from-children gulf. When Julio was in a meeting, he was in a meeting. But I've been on panels at international literary festivals talking about new trends in narrative non-fiction, while simultaneously mulling over ways to contrive a child's favourite stuffed toy away for long enough to give it a wash.

There was the parenting nitty-gritty gulf. Julio never stayed up unable to sleep, making lists in his head about school snacks, after-school activity scheduling, birthday invite making, goody bag shopping and the like.

For the days, or more rarely, the weeks, that I would be away from the family, travelling on work, Julio ostensibly held the fort. And it is true that when I returned, the house had not burnt down, nor had Ishaan broken any limbs, or swallowed poison.

But raisins had invariably not been sent on raisin day, swimming classes were missed, cookies were eaten for breakfast, school correspondence remained unanswered, and teeth occasionally went unbrushed.

Julio's response to these lapses being pointed out would be to shrug his shoulders. 'Relax,' he'd say. 'Everything is fine.' True enough, but not enough. Being a parent is about so much more than big-picture well-being. It is about the infinite, day-to-day details of drying tears, cleaning bottoms, establishing relations with classmate's parents, keeping vaccinations up to date, planning the next day's nutritious, but tasty, school lunch, finding the time to get haircuts, clipping nails, finding lost toys, and on and on.

For years our marital home was rocked with strife over childcare divisions, and nothing irritated me more than when Julio smirked about how he was a visionary interested in broad developments and goals, while I was a right-hand 'man' who worried about the details. The comment was meant to needle me, and it worked, because I hadn't wanted this managerial role. At least, I had never envisaged I would be so alone in it. I'd had it thrust upon me by motherhood and a 'visionary' father who abandoned me to get on with it. And I couldn't refuse. I didn't have a wife.

I tried over the years to develop a 'Julio' attitude. I made mindful attempts to not think about my son while working. I actively tried to switch off; to just let him be while I got on with more 'important' things. It never worked. So how did my husband do it?

Did he really not give a hoot about the web of scheduling and other logistics that consumed so much of my time, morphing me, like most mothers, into the unacknowledged CEO of a small and medium enterprise? Or was the real reason why Julio could disconnect because he knew I was meticulously taking care of the quotidian drudge? The occasions that I was away from the family were transient enough to indulge in benign negligence.

Uncombed hair and absent snack boxes can be tolerated easily for a couple of days. Teachers are understanding knowing that 'mom' is travelling. And the child probably enjoys the relative chaos in the short term. It is remarkable that this scenario reads like a set-piece family comedy from circa 1950, where the plot involves 'Father' realizing just how tough a job 'Mother' has when he takes over domestic responsibilities for a day, only to make a humorous hash of it, until the indulgent mom returns to restore order at home. Despite the passing of decades, the slog of the feminist movement, and my own successful career, our multicultural and thoroughly twenty-first-century family was not, at core, all that different.

What would Julio have been like were he a single dad? Would he, by nature, have remained as detached, happy to play with Ishaan, but loathe to make those dreadful 'to do' lists I was always composing? Or in the absence of a woman (wife, mother, mother-in-law) to rely on, would his emotional make-up change to match that of anxious, guilt-ridden, detail-oriented mothers everywhere?

The answer to this question is seminal to society's ideal of gender-associated roles and relations, in the private and public spheres. Is the reason why most women appear so much more emotionally and mentally fused with their children, than men genetic? After all, such differences are unarguably known to exist in other species of animals.

Male polar bears eat cubs even as female bears aggressively defend their offspring for years. I was often put in mind of this when observing how Julio would casually wolf down the last piece of honey toast at the breakfast table, even as Ishaan wailed for it. 'I'm bigger than you,' he'd say with a shrug, 'so, I need more food.' In contrast, even though I wasn't a self-sacrificing type by nature, I found it physically impossible to deprive my child of nutritious food, even at the cost of going hungry myself.

If men are biologically unable to change and become more like women in their emotional response to parenthood, women need to work on acceptance, and give up unrealistic expectations of equality in parenting. The focus of public policy should be on finding ways to manage the tension between this unavoidable gender inequality at home, and the possibility of professional equality in the public sphere. In this scenario, the onus for 'having it all' falls squarely on women, as they must expect, and accept, it to be harder for them, if they choose to work. This is in fact the status quo at present, where more women than ever before have careers, even as their role as primary caregivers for the family remains largely unaltered.

However, if the attitudes of men to childcare are learnt behaviour, many fathers are simply enjoying the fruits of socially condoned laziness. In this scenario, social and gender policy should not be so focused, as at present, on women in the workplace, but on men in the family. The key challenge in this case lies in devising encouragement for men to take on more responsibility for bringing up their kids. If successful, women would automatically find it easier to pursue other choices.

When Ishaan was around six weeks old I received an invite from a Chinese writer friend for a dinner at her home in honour of the celebrated Indian intellectual, Pankaj Mishra. I managed to find a moment to succumb to the excitement of the prospect of meeting one of my writerly idols. Mishra's 1995 travelogue of small-town India, *Butter Chicken in Ludhiana,* had long been an inspiration to me. The manner in which he'd combined an authentically Indian sensibility with the critical dispassion of an outsider while tackling his subject, had been unique at the time. His reputation had gone global in the years since, and my friend said he was currently in Beijing to research long-form pieces on China, for a big-name US publication.

At this point, I hadn't been away from the baby for more than an hour since we'd returned home from the hospital. Ishaan was in the midst of the worst of the colic, with purple-faced crying jags that could only be partially soothed by hours of creative calisthenics on my part. The idea of going to a dinner party to meet a writer felt about as realistic as an offer to dine with the tooth fairy on the moon. Fine food and intelligent conversation belonged to other people's lives.

But, Julio immediately intervened, insisting that I go. Auntie Mei was recruited into staying on in the evening to assist, so that I could escape the universe of pacifiers and sterilizers to sally forth into the glamorous alternative world of No-Baby. 'Switch off,' Julio told me airily. 'Don't worry. Just enjoy yourself.'

Of course, I couldn't switch off wholly, and for much of the evening I had the kind of nervous gnawing in the pit of my stomach that goes along with the night before a high-school mathematics exam. But regardless, it was one of the most memorable two hours of my life, transported as I had been into a room where no one was screaming and where my breasts could remain resting inside my clothes.

At one point I found myself swaying rhythmically from side to side while talking to a friend. After weeks of the constant motion needed to soothe Ishaan I found it difficult to just stand still, sipping a drink. Rocking had become my de facto state of being. For the millionth time I wondered if the baby was OK.

Then, an hour into the party, it happened. I found myself next to the great and bearded Pankaj Mishra, who was most genial and seemed genuinely interested in what I had to say. I nattered away for a few minutes, feeling blissfully untethered, before the

Cinderella realization that my time was up struck me. I needed to return home for a feeding. I made my excuses to get away, at which point the great Mishra unexpectedly asked if I'd be up for meeting him for a coffee later in the week. Um, would a dolphin be up for a swim? Would a mouse be up for some cheese? Would a mother be up for a lie-in?

I nodded a ready, heady, assent and we arranged to meet a few days later at a tea house located in Ritan Park, one of central Beijing's historic gardens. I spent the intervening days in a frenzy of preparation. Every morning I pumped for hours, squeezing out a few millilitres of milk at a time, which when combined made up a gloriously full bottle for Ishaan to drink while I was at my Mishra tête-à-tête.

I repeatedly made Auntie Mei promise that she would call me if the crying got too much for her to handle. (Throughout the colic I remained convinced that Ishaan was unsafe in another person's care because no one but I could tolerate the crying without attempting to murder him. In retrospect, I was probably the only person driven to the point of contemplating murder or suicide, by his yowling, because the crying didn't appear to affect other people as keenly as it did me. There are, in fact, several scientific studies establishing that mothers react to their infant's distress more strongly than others, the result of a 'biological adaptation to specific demands associated with successful infant care'.)[2]

On the big day Auntie Mei shooed me out of the house as Ishaan took a rare peaceful nap. Soon I found myself seated next to Pankaj, soaking in the calm of the tea house like a cat basking in the winter sun. The clatter of cups, the hiss of steaming water and the crackle of sunflower seeds being split open – the sounds rippled like wind dancing on willow trees. It was scented balm to my colic-ripped soul. Pankaj was as erudite as one had imagined. He made insightful observations, asked piercing questions, and nodded thoughtfully at my answers. What a privilege, I thought to myself, to have unexpectedly stumbled upon this sliver of pre-baby life.

I mentioned, shyly, about what a treat it was to have this break from baby care. 'You have a baby?' Pankaj asked, looking slightly uncomfortable in the way great men do when talking about children. I smiled, and nodded. 'So do I,' he replied in his gruff baritone. I couldn't have been more taken aback if he had announced that he was the Queen of Sheba.

What did he mean that he had a baby too? What was he doing traipsing around China writing pieces for *The New York Times*, when he had a small child at home? Why was I marvelling at this tiny chink of normality in my post-partum life of burp cloths and bottles, while Pankaj's post-partum life consisted of global flânerie, big thoughts, and tea house rendezvous?

It was at that moment I realized that, while there may have been a many-shaped gulf between Julio and me on the parenting experience, the chasm separating male and female writers was of another order altogether. From the day that Ishaan was born to the day I am writing these words, I have worked in open-doored chaos, stealing sentences in between settling sibling spats, sneaking in edits while supervising homework, and forcing my mind to seek silence within my head, as a maelstrom of toddler tantrums and playful shrieking engulfed my body.

The great Mishra in the meantime divides his time between London, where his family resides, and Mashobra, a peaceful hill station in India so conducive to writing it would make a novelist out of a chartered accountant. Pankaj is hardly alone in enjoying this male authorial privilege. He's probably a great father too. But a mother who spent as much time away from her child, writing books, would automatically be a bad mother. And this would be an internal label as much as an external one.

Having had my own kids I also believe that only a rare mother would choose to leave small children for long periods of time to pursue a professional life. Even in the case of a supportive spouse, the loss of time with the children would be too high a price to pay for most. So, do women just love their children more than men? Or have they been socially conditioned to value child rearing over other markers in their life? I was back to that impenetrable riddle.

Years later, I met Pankaj for the third time, at a book event of his, in Delhi. We had been in occasional email contact in the intervening years and he was encouraging of my work. I was grateful to him and continued to admire his writing. We had a short chat before he went on stage. He asked about my son, and I inquired after his daughter, who, he said, was doing well. After a moment's hesitation I asked him point blank how he managed to travel as much as he did with such a young child.

Pankaj didn't bat an eye as he replied that he had a 'good support system'. 'You mean you have a wife,' I retorted. Not for the first, or last, time I wished I had a wife too.

3

SLEEP

SEPTEMBER–DECEMBER 2008, BEIJING

I didn't have a wife. But I did have a husband. A much loved one. All I wanted of this husband, or so I told him often, was more of his involvement in the everyday details. And so I learnt the truth behind another hoary cliché: be careful what you wish for; it may come true.

Six years on it is easy for me to insert myself in Julio's shoes. He had taken a month off from work to find himself essentially superfluous in a home filled with a baby's screaming and his wild-haired wife's accusations about the unfairness of everything.

Ishaan had lived and formed inside my body for months. I had a sense of ownership over the baby that was physical and fierce. As a result, even as I railed at Julio for not doing enough, I didn't give him the freedom to actually do much. I constantly corrected the way he held the baby or the comforting techniques he attempted to use. I did this because I knew, for example, that, Ishaan preferred being carried upright, to the sideways cradle Julio tended to adopt. But for Julio my constant interfering must have been dispiriting.

Eventually, he turned to the one activity that gave him a

simultaneous sense of control and involvement: research. And as all baby-related roads lead to the mother's breasts, Julio soon fancied himself as an expert on my breasts and what I should be doing with them.

He would stay up nights reading the blogs of assorted lactation consultants and scribbling neat notes for me to peruse. He sent out orders on Amazon for fennel seed supplements, a known herbal lactation aid. He suggested I try getting a prescription for domperidone, a medication often used to ease symptoms of nausea and vomiting, but also shown to increase milk production in some women.

But when Julio recommended that I set the alarm clock so as to wake every two hours through the night in order to attach my chest to a pump for a twenty-minute milking session, thereby 'stimulating' my supply, I'd heard just about enough.

At one level I realized Julio was only trying to 'help' a situation – low milk supply – that I myself was agonizing about. But I hated what I perceived as his interference in what was a deeply private matter. The reality was that I wanted him involved, but on my own terms.

His evangelizing about breastfeeding was not the kind of support I craved from him during those early months. It only seemed to drive the stake of failure deeper into my heart. What I wanted was affirmation that I was a good mother despite problems with my milk supply. Julio's efforts to 'help' merely amounted to another finger pointing at me. Suffice it to say I did not take kindly to the little post-its with lactation tips that I found on my bedside table in the mornings. In fact, I took some satisfaction in shredding these to bits and tossing them in the general direction of the dustbin while yelling at my husband to *leave me alone.*

Of course, only a few hours earlier I had been yelling at him to be more concerned. Given how emotional, contradictory, disorienting and just huge motherhood is, mixed feelings and their garbled communication are par for the course. The problem is that fathers don't always understand. In many ways the contradictory signals that Julio got from me only caused him to hold back further.

He found himself the target of my ire regardless of whether he tried to get 'involved' or just stayed away. Absenting himself was the easier option. And so a pattern was set for our journey as parents that proved difficult to break.

But, in the meantime, as Ishaan's colic continued unabated, I was doing my own research and coming up with the same findings that Julio was. Although no one could authoritatively explain colic, there was a widespread assumption that formula milk irritated the baby's bowels, causing the crying. Adding fuel to my angst, a major baby milk scandal had hit China just a few days before Ishaan was born.

As many as twenty-one Chinese infant formula companies were found to have adulterated their products with chemicals like melamine. By November 2008, the contaminated milk had affected at least 300,000 babies, with six having died from kidney-related problems and 54,000 hospitalized. The formula we were 'topping up' Ishaan with was imported and unconnected to any Chinese company, but the milk scandal deepened my guilt of not exclusively breastfeeding my baby.

Egged on by Julio, I resolved to try and quit the formula once and for all. The first stop in this quest was at a local La Leche League meeting. The La Leche League is a breastfeeding support group that operates around the world, and its Beijing chapter met once a week at the same hospital where I'd given birth.

I arrived at the meeting wearing Ishaan in a sling and found myself sitting in a circle with an assorted cast of pregnant and lactating women, most of whom were expats. The meeting was led by a diminutive, mousy-haired American, out of whose lap an enormous child hopped on and off through the meeting, at one point nuzzling up to her breast and taking a long drink.

The 'leader' began with assurances that all women have an adequate milk supply and went on to talk about several myths related to breastfeeding, including the suggestions that breastfeeding women could not drink coffee or the occasional glass of wine; or that formula-fed babies slept longer; or that breastfeeding mothers could not work. 'Believe in your breasts,' she exhorted. 'Nature will not let you down.'

I felt buoyed on a cloud of milky optimism. The feeling of being immersed in a room full of maternal warmth unshackled something within me, and in an act that felt liberating and defiant, I pulled out a mammary and gave Ishaan free rein at it. This was immediately met with much approving cooing and clucking. One expectant mom beside me was positively dewy-eyed as she exclaimed that the sight of me nursing was 'just beautiful'. 'It's my greatest dream', she sighed, 'to breastfeed my baby like you are.'

A dam burst within me. Here I was being upheld as a paragon of motherhood, when in fact I was a formula-topping-up charlatan. 'I've made a huge mistake,' I moaned and began to gabble confessions like a lapsed Catholic on her deathbed.

The whole miserable story came tumbling out from that first bottle of formula that I'd allowed Ishaan in hospital, to the violent colic that had driven me to born-again La Leche-ism.

The approbation I had evoked in the beginning was now replaced with consternation. The meeting leader shooed her well-fed three-year-old off to play and turned to me, eyes burning with pious intensity. Yes, I had made an error, but I could build up my breast milk supply to 'normal', she said, if I decided to make a full-time commitment. 'Believe in your breasts,' she repeated.

I needed to take a 'nursing holiday'. To stay in bed for a few days with the baby, without any distractions, except for feeding on demand, round the clock. Every minute on the breast would build up my supply. As for the colic, my baby was obviously sensitive, so that I'd need to avoid consuming dairy (yoghurt, cheese, milk, butter), garlic, onions, chocolate, coffee, alcohol, spice, spinach, cauliflower, tomatoes, peanuts, shellfish. There were other foods too, which she couldn't remember off hand, but promised to send me an email later.

I returned home feeling doomed but determined, like Frodo Baggins of the *Lord of the Rings* trudging towards Modor. This was also an apt analogy to describe how much I was enjoying the whole motherhood experience. I took the breastfeeding 'holiday'. I consumed fenugreek and domperidone by the gallon. I pumped and pumped. And I stopped eating all dairy.

The results were not encouraging. Ishaan continued to cry for hours a day and my milk supply – as judged by my efforts at pumping – remained stubbornly put. I took Ishaan to the hospital to have him weighed every few days. He was not gaining adequate weight and even as I desperately muttered to myself to 'believe in my breasts', I was finding it very hard to do so.

The weeks ticked by in a blur. Terrorists attacked Mumbai and laid siege to the Taj Mahal Hotel. My thirty-third birthday came and went. I gave up exclusive breastfeeding once again, allowing Ishaan a bottle or two a day. Four things saved me from complete despair: Harvey Carp, Auntie Mei, the Internet and Bob Marley.

Harvey Karp was the most productive discovery of Julio's research efforts. A celebrity American paediatrician, Karp claimed to have discovered that 'colic' had nothing to do with digestive disorders but was rather an expression of the need some babies had for a fourth trimester. The three trimesters in-utero were not sufficient for these babies. Their nervous systems remained immature and they felt thrust out into the world three months too early. A rude disruption was caused when they were forced to exchange the dark, loud, constantly moving place that was the womb, for a world of light, stillness and quiet. It was this disruption that colicky babies spent their days (and nights) protesting against. In short, what these babies really wanted was a return to the comfort they had known within their mothers.

The solution, according to Karp, was to swaddle a baby tightly, subject her to loud 'white noise' (the womb was apparently full of very noisy whooshing and gurgling sounds), and swing her about constantly. We immediately set about trying to follow this advice and it was miraculous. Immobilized within a swaddling blanket and subject to the loud sound of a hair dryer, little Ishaan would simply switch off and shut down. A period of peaceful sleep ensued. But the moment one dared to put off the overworked hair dryer, he was back up and yelling.

Our nanny, Auntie Mei, was perturbed by the whole business. Denying all empirical evidence to the contrary, she insisted that the hair dryer could not possibly help the baby to sleep. I agreed that it was counter-intuitive – it was certainly not my preferred aural backdrop for slumber – but it worked for Ishaan. Mei remained mutinous.

She was, in fact, suspicious of the entire concept of 'colic'. 'In China there is no such thing,' she said sniffily, when we tried explaining the term to her, as it had been explained to us. In China, we were to discover, much was different. For example, there was no distinction between the word for 'burp' and 'hiccup'. Both were simply called '*da ge*'. We tried asking Auntie Mei how the Chinese could tell the two apart in the absence of different words to describe them. 'But they're the same thing,' she replied firmly. 'Hiccups are just more intense than a burp.' It was a bit confusing since this statement went something like '*Da ge* are just more intense than *da ge*'.

Auntie Mei tended to display the kind of brutal honesty that I had often observed in China over the years. I remember meeting my students at the Beijing Broadcasting Institute for the first time when I began teaching English there in 2002. I had asked the students to introduce themselves and a rather portly youth had stood up and announced, 'My name is Fat because I am fat.' While I had hurried to assure him (falsely) that this was not the case, his classmates had merely nodded slowly in agreement, at what they'd obviously considered to be no more than a straightforward statement of fact.

Six years on we found ourselves at the receiving end of several similar truthful punches, in the company of Auntie Mei. One morning, Julio and I decided to take the bull by the horns, and force Mei into compliance with Harvey Karp. Julio had acquired a Karp video complete with Chinese subtitles, in which the doctor, radiating authority in a white coat, explained his theory with impeccable logic, in addition to some practical demonstrations of his magic touch in calming bawling babes. As far as Julio and I were concerned, the DVD was irrefutable proof, if any was needed in addition to Ishaan's response to the hair dryer, of the infallibility of Karp.

We invited Auntie Mei to join us for a viewing. She was reluctant, it being her tendency to give all advice of non-Chinese origin short shrift, but we eventually persuaded her to watch with us by bribing her with an especially fragrant cup of jasmine tea.

We sat down in the living room, on the sofa opposite the TV screen, Julio sandwiched between Auntie Mei and me. After a few minutes of watching, Mei got up and moved away from her original seat to an armchair at the far end of the room. Assuming she had shifted out of deference to their difference in status, Julio hastened to assure her. 'Please don't feel awkward,' he said. 'You are very welcome to sit next to me.'

'Oh, I know,' came the reply. 'It's just that your feet smell.'

Auntie Mei was also less than sensitive about my milk supply angst. 'You don't have enough,' she roughly diagnosed the week we returned from the hospital. As I sat pumping away miserably, she launched into stories of her own copious lactation. 'When my baby was born I had so much milk, it would just run out of my breasts and soak my clothes no matter what,' she regularly reminisced, completely oblivious that such revelations had me running into my room to sob into a pillow. 'I had enough milk to feed two or three babies,' the relentless memoirs would continue, even from behind closed doors.

Auntie Li, Mei's sister-in-law, was more sympathetic. 'I didn't have enough (milk) for mine,' she told me conspiratorially while urging her standard small black chicken soup on me – which was apparently a lactation aid in addition to curing all other known human ailments. 'My husband was angry because formula was expensive. But what could I do?'

I came to clutch at Li, and especially the poker-faced Mei, like a drowning sailor to a piece of driftwood. Disoriented by motherhood, aggravated by Julio and distant from my childhood friends and family, it was Mei's skills with Ishaan that allowed a semblance of sanity to persist in the house. She spent hours soothing him and helped to bathe him even as he resisted red-faced and screeching. She told me that crying was good exercise for a baby's lungs.

'Chinese babies cry too,' she once said, upon finding me pacing up and down a room with an inconsolable Ishaan, a broken look on my face. It was the kindest thing anyone could have said to me at that moment, especially because it wasn't meant as a kindness. It was just a truth.

Mei would also sit up in the evenings with me, as I nursed Ishaan, and talk about her childhood in impoverished Anhui province. Things used to be terribly hard in the Maoist heyday. There was no electricity, and food was scarce. People had to catch and eat rats. But she was happy enough. Because she could read and write, she was appointed by the village committee to teach at the school. It was a job that came with respect.

I found listening to these simple stories of her childhood profoundly soothing. They provided some perspective. And they also allowed me to just think about other lives, in other times, for a few moments.

My other 'saviour' was ironically also the source of much of my stress: the Internet. It was online that I encountered that deluge of guilt-inducing parenting articles that threaten to drown every new mother with a Wi-Fi connection. But it was also in cyberspace that I finally found the kind of support I needed, but did not receive from my corporeal context.

After weeks of meeting doctors who told me to 'relax' and wait it out, a husband who suggested medication to induce lactation, a La Leche League leader who recommended breastfeeding holidays, a mother who lived in another country, and a group of friends who were chary of committing to pets leave alone babies, I stumbled upon the 'Fussy Baby and Colic Support Group', online.

This was a website run by a mother based in British Colombia, Canada, a place I would be hard placed to identify on a map. Yet, over the next few months, it became a refuge. It was here that I found mothers (it was a very uncommon dad whom I encountered on the site) with the same stories as mine. These were not stories fluttering with coos and sighs and lovely baby smells, these were tales bursting with screams and panic. In the end, it was all I needed: just the knowledge that I was not alone in the world; that there were other mothers desperately plugging in hair dryers to get their 'angels' to sleep too.

I read about moms who hadn't slept through a night in over a year. And I learnt about babies who fussed on their tummies and those that fussed on their backs. I heard about babies who refused all foods and babies who wouldn't stop eating. There was this whole granular, complex world out there that had been a wholly blank space in my consciousness until I had Ishaan. How did one manage to live a successful and busy life for thirty-three years without having encountered it?

I'd learnt mathematics, history and geography in school. I'd studied Aristotle and Kant, Foucault and Baudrillard at university. But although there was much that I knew about humankind's collective inquiries into epistemology and ontology, no one ever taught me anything about babies. Nor had I absorbed such knowledge unconsciously either, never having been exposed to baby care. Perhaps there had been a more fertile, birth-rate-friendly time when child rearing was part of the weft of daily life. But this was no longer the case for urban, middle-class folk like me.

What does it say about contemporary society that it can churn out a person who can speak foreign languages, dance the tango, be paid to lecture on Chinese politics, discuss how far the taxation policies instituted by the Count Duke Olivares had contributed to the decline of seventeenth-century Spain, and yet had no clue how to feed and entertain a baby all day long. It became clear to me that I was essentially a 'man'. I knew all about the public world of 'work' but nothing about the 'womanly' art of nurturing children.

The online sites I subsequently found were like the alphabet to an illiterate. It was through them that I was able to make some sense of what was otherwise the pure bewilderment of life with an infant. I rarely contributed to the discussions on the site; but I read what other women had to say about sleep, nutrition, cutting teeth, tummy time and drool, with enormous relief and the kind of rapt attention that I'd reserved for great literature in my pre-baby life. This was the cyber village that helped me to raise Ishaan that first year.

The fact that I was now spending a majority of my time in female company, either with Auntie Mei, or online with the Canadian mommies, underlined how 'male' my life had been hitherto. The first 'adult' parties I'd attended in Beijing were at the homes of Indian embassy officials. These were invariably married men with children. Julio and I would cross over from our just-out-of-university lives into these bastions of traditional domesticity for an evening, and come out shaking our heads in mirth and condescension.

At these parties it was as though an invisible purdah divided the room, with women discussing children and schools on one side, and men pondering politics and the economy on the other. I was invariably the only woman on the male end, given that I stridently occupied the public realm of ideas and action, and scorned the domestic and family-oriented world that so many women seemed lost in, if I thought about it at all.

Once Ishaan was born, men, other than Julio, more or less disappeared from my lives. There was nothing that made a man vanish quicker than talk about breast milk supply, which had become my primary preoccupation. Unable to read or even absorb much news of the wider world given my levels of exhaustion, I had begun to find long and involved conversations about nap-inducing techniques, which were immediately pertinent to my life, far more absorbing than discussions about the reform of Chinese state-owned enterprises and the like.

Now, when we attended those Indian embassy parties, I was no longer to be found quaffing beers with the 'boys', shooting the breeze about energy policy and great power rivalry. These were matters that seemed inane, if not narcissistic. It was the women with their helpful recipes for weaning foods, and assurances that every trial I was facing with Ishaan was just a phase, whom I came to appreciate.

I was struck by how almost all the men, of varying nationalities, present on these occasions, were fathers, and yet rarely joined in the discussions about children. Even through the fog of early motherhood I was frustrated by this. The gendered divisions on display at these parties were not the outcome of biology, but were merely an unapologetic display of male privilege. They were demonstrations of the bald fact that even today men could just leave the gathering of child-rearing information to their wives. They had wives. The wives, whether or not they also worked outside the home, were stuck with husbands.

There was one father, an old friend from university in Oxford, who reconnected with me around this time on Facebook. A former molecular plant biologist, the friend was now a stay-at-home dad bringing up two little girls. His was the sole male voice with similar preoccupations to mine, through this period. And he had some top advice on everything from diapering to sleep. My friend was a tall and strapping lad; a former rower and athlete; a paragon of masculinity. But because he was now the primary caregiver for his children, he was as embroiled in the details of babyhood as I was.

This had nothing to do with his genetic make-up but with a choice he had made. And most men did not make this choice. Nor were they required to or even nudged towards making that choice by the workplace, government policy or the education system.

My final salvation from colic dystopia was Bob Marley's '*Buffalo Soldier*'. Amongst the mountains of baby-related information I spent the day trudging through, I came across a 'trick' recommended for colicky infants, to do with reggae music. The offbeat rhythm of the music soothed them, an article claimed. I scurried off to dust off my 'Best of Bob Marley' CD.

'*Wai yai yai; wai yai yai yai*,' the refrain for '*Buffalo Soldier*' sounded too much like a baby crying for comfort, when suddenly I noticed something. Ishaan had stopped screaming. In fact his lips were making a most unusual, stretched-out shape. It was definitely a smile. His first smile. I held him close to me and felt my muscles relax into his soft, baby loveliness. Loveliness? That was not a sentiment I had associated much with the baby, yet there it unmistakably was. Ishaan was lovely. And Bob Marley rocked.

In the coming days I filled the house with music. We danced to Dire Straits, swayed to Bach and stamped through flamenco. Even Auntie Mei, at first predictably sceptical at this thoroughly un-Chinese behaviour, came around, and one day I caught her doing the twist, baby clasped to the hip, Chubby Checker belting out a number in the background.

By late December 2008, when Ishaan was around three months old, I decided to stop breastfeeding once and for all, and switch wholly to formula. It was a decision that brought me the greatest relief I'd ever felt, until that point in my life. The dratted breast pump was put away and my fenugreek supplements retired. The fact that I could detach from the baby for more than a couple of hours at a go was wildly liberating. I felt myself breathing and realized I'd been holding my breath in a three-month-long pause of anxiety. I went to the spa for a massage that left me teary with pleasure. I read a book. I gargled in cheese, cappuccinos, and every other kind of dairy product I could lay my hands on.

Ishaan began to gain weight, his cheeks filling out into the kind of baby puffiness that aunties globally find it impossible to resist pulling. He cried for fewer hours a day as well. Yet, he remained unable to sleep for more than a couple of hours at a stretch. Even though he was exhausted, he seemed to fight closing his eyes. When he finally succumbed to slumber he'd twitch about in his sleep like a pugilist pacing up and down a fighting ring in preparation for his next bout.

I switched my Internet research from feeding issues to sleep. The Fussy Baby site was full of moms claiming they hadn't slept through a single night in upwards of eighteen months. I was filled with dread. The three months of sleep deprivation I had suffered had sufficed to turn me into a bad-tempered witch. What would eighteen months do to me? Would there even be any 'me' left at the end of it all?

As I googled 'infant insomnia' or 'baby fights sleep', I found thousands of pages of information on sleep apnoea, underlying neurological disorders, allergies and other bone-chilling explanations for why some infants could not sleep. Others focused on the things parents were doing wrong; well-intentioned actions that actually discouraged their children from learning how to sleep.

Never rock your child to sleep. Put him down in his cot when he is drowsy but still awake was the most common advice. This was so that the infant would not awake in the middle of the night wondering why he was no longer being rocked in his parent's arms, but lying still in a cot instead. Awareness of his sleep surroundings would ensure a baby continued to sleep through the night, rather than rousing to full alertness during one of the fleeting awakenings that everyone experiences as sleep cycles wax and wane.

As with so much parenting advice, this was obviously not applicable to a colicky baby. It would have been easier to go to sleep cuddling a full-grown tiger than putting Ishaan down in his cot when he was in the 'drowsy but still awake' state. We usually had to bounce him up and down while performing deep knee bends for at least twenty minutes even after he first closed his eyes to ensure very deep sleep before laying him on any flat surface. Put him down too quickly and all the preceding aerobics would come to naught; he'd be up before I could even make it to the door, screaming his outrage at being asked to sleep.

Julio and I were plagued by existential questions. How could a human child have such denuded instincts of self-preservation? On a website dedicated to horses I read that foals were usually cavorting around independently within an hour of being born (they took their first nap within two hours). But our baby could not hold up his head, could not move, could not eliminate bodily waste cleanly, and could not sleep without enormous parental efforts. One assumed that evolutionary processes equipped human babies with compensating characteristics for their overwhelming helplessness. Here is where 'cuteness' came into play, allowing babies to demand impossible feats of their parents by compensating them with cute smiles and burbling coos.

But what of a colicky infant? The only reward awaiting a parent in this instance was shrieking and sleep deprivation. How did these babies survive in other times, where parents had fewer resources? Was there no colic amongst cavemen? Amongst the Aztecs? Mei certainly claimed it didn't exist in China.

There is considerable literature on colic that claims it is a 'Western' invention and that 'traditional' cultures where mothers wear their children close to the skin twenty-four hours a day, breastfeed constantly and respond to their cries immediately, have no knowledge of it. This sounded like bunkum. Even Mei had admitted that Chinese kids cried.

The import of much of this research, it seemed to me, was to blame the 'modern' mother for wanting a life where she could put down her infant for a few hours and expect some shut eye. Surely there are plenty of instances in 'traditional' societies where mothers are malnourished, so that their breast milk does not supply optimal nourishment; where they are distracted by the needs of numerous other children and depleted by the necessity of earning a wage. I'd seen plenty of examples in India of babies being left behind with barely competent older siblings, or physically weak grandparents for hours on end. Perhaps some of these infants cried less because they had been trained by neglect that it was of no use.

This left me with a conundrum. Was my baby crying because I was not doing enough to meet his needs or because I was doing too much? Julio had come to believe the latter. He was constantly haranguing me about the efforts I put into keeping Ishaan calm and sleeping. 'Just put him down and let him cry for a while,' Julio would tell me after having watched me bounce, sing and sway Ishaan for hours into the early morning.

These exhortations made me furious. The idea of just leaving the baby to bawl was like asking me to chop off a body part. Perhaps it was biology.[1] But it was also that I had come to believe that I had already failed my baby on so many counts. I had failed to exclusively breastfeed; I had failed to have a happy and content baby; I had failed to enjoy my baby. What Julio was asking me to do, to just put Ishaan down and walk away, would have been the greatest failure of all.

And I couldn't believe that my husband dared to suggest it. It felt like an unhelpful, lazy, idea that stemmed from some kind of male callousness that I couldn't even fathom. I had dark thoughts about male polar bears and Komodo dragons eating their offspring.

It was around this time that I encountered the 'attachment parenting' philosophy espoused by William (Bill) Sears, another American paediatrician of considerable repute. Attachment parenting advises co-sleeping (sleeping in the same bed as the baby) and breastfeeding on demand. Mothers are told to change their expectations of their lives after giving birth; to realize and embrace the fact that they will no longer sleep well for a few years. Instead, they are advised to immediately, and sensitively, respond to their babies' needs, holding them, stroking them and singing to them. In the absence of this total devotion to the child, a mother risks causing emotional and developmental damage to the baby.

Attachment parenting has a wide following around the world. The description above might be somewhat reductive, but holds generally true to the spirit of the theory. It is essentially a verbal elaboration of the kind of mother-and-baby pictures that are on abundant display in glossy magazines, selling everything from moisturizing lotions to towels. The emphasis is on the gentle, fluffy, glowing. The look on the mother's face in these shots is invariably infused with a transcendent joy. They convey the message that women somehow ascend to a different plane once they become mothers: and there they should stay, bathed in God's grace and the approval of attachment parenting advocates.

'Scheduling', or the idea that a mother should decide in advance when to feed her baby or put him to sleep, is like garlic to a vampire for attachment-parenting enthusiasts. Instead they vigorously espouse allowing the baby to decide when it wants to eat or sleep, regardless of any inconveniences this might cause the mother or the family.

There is also scant room for the father in this philosophy, with its overwhelming emphasis on breastfeeding. This is the first text I came across when I googled 'attachment parenting, role of dads (or at least the first one where the link worked. Dr Sears' page devoted to fathers fittingly refused to open):

> 'Practically speaking, Dad can do a lot: in addition to nurturing Mom, he can do everything other than nursing. Dad can change diapers, bathe, carry, hold, rock, sing, read books, play, and more. He can build the baby's trust and bond with him. *However, most of the time his contact with the baby needs to be in the presence of*

> *Mom* until it is obvious that the baby delights in spending time alone with him ... *If too often when the baby sees Dad, he loses Mom, he may resent and fear him, and try to avoid him. Fathers need to be the connection, not the disconnection.*'

Even when the father is 'involved', the mother must remain physically present. There is no escape for women from the heaven of motherhood.

Six years on, I can see attachment parenting as a regressive and gendered theory, cut of the same cultural cloth that has created the cult of the child – where children are worshipped as the centre of their parents', and, in particular, mothers', existence.

The fact is that mothers come in all shapes, sizes and temperaments. But I am yet to come across one who doesn't respond to her baby's needs sensitively and as promptly as she can. Sometimes, however, she might need to go to the bathroom before settling down to breastfeed, or to answer the telephone and talk to a friend in need for a while. She might even have to finish a work-related deadline, because she might actually want to work on something other than catering to her baby.

As a first-time mother to a cranky baby, however, I was vulnerable to the guilt implicitly manufactured by Sears's writings, which I purchased and consumed voraciously. They resulted in much self-hate. If the only way to 'bond' with my baby was to spend all twenty-four hours attending to his never-ending needs, with a smile on my lips, calm in my heart and no other expectations of my life, I realized I'd made a terrible mistake. I was not cut out to be a mother. But now that I was one, I had to face the consequences. In order to make sure my baby was happy, I had to kill my own needs. I would never be happy myself again. But how did this matter if my baby grew up to be well adjusted and healthy?

In hindsight these feelings seem laughably overwrought. In

the intervening six years I have lived through so many phases with both my children that the great truth I have learnt is that everything passes. Julio had tried to get me to see this early on. I remember him attempting to cheer me up after I'd managed to wrestle the baby to sleep following a six-hour crying jag. 'I'm sure by the time he goes for a college interview he'll have stopped crying,' Julio had joked. But I hadn't smiled in response.

The question remained: *when* would things change? And would I have been changed irrevocably by then? The answers, of course, were: 'soon', and 'yes – it's called growing up'.

I continued my desperate research online and eventually stumbled across a clinic that specialized in paediatric sleeping disorders. The only catch was that it was in faraway Brussels, the capital of Belgium. Serendipitously, however, having passed the rigorous examination for the European Union civil service, Julio had begun to look for jobs in precisely that city. Brussels was host to the European Commission's headquarters. And although no job confirmation had come through as yet, we knew it was only a matter of time before we'd be saying goodbye to China, and heading Brussels-ward to sleep-clinic deliverance.

It was thus that Dr Goldman entered our lives. The doctor was a Belgian who lived in Beijing, and was the paediatrician for the son of friends. When the friends, a well-built Scottish–Norwegian couple, visited Goldman to discuss their concerns over the weight issues of their chubby, happy, ten-month-old who already clocked in at 10 kg, the doctor had sniffed at the podgy babe and in a thick French accent suggested that 'perhaps it is genetic!'

Julio and I arrived at our appointment with Goldman, clutching Ishaan and gabbling about sleep disorders as the doctor trained his sceptical stare at us. Our cause was not helped by the fact that Ishaan had frustratingly morphed into an angelic cherub. Suddenly, the epitome of serenity, he looked up at the doctor from behind flirtatiously long eyelashes with friendly curiosity.

I anxiously explained Ishaan's sleeping issues in detail: how he fought sleep and rarely managed to stay asleep for any length of time; how he was in constant motion even when his eyes were closed, and how he cried and raged all the time. I paused for breath and Ishaan interjected with a gurgle, as if mildly amused at his mother's hysterical ranting. 'Oh come on! Just one blood-curdling scream to show the doctor,' I found myself mentally urging the baby. But he remained stubbornly good-natured.

I turned back to Goldman and admitted that I wasn't sure if Ishaan had infant apnoea or any other physiological problem. We obviously needed to get a professional sleep study done. I explained how we expected to be moving to Brussels soon, and had heard about a clinic that specialized in paediatric sleep disorders. Being from Brussels himself, could the doctor give us a reference for a sleep specialist there?

There was a long pause as Goldman looked at us like we were a particularly exotic species of insect. When he finally spoke, his French accent somehow added to his authoritativeness. 'This problem you talk about,' he said with a dismissive gesture, 'is not a very uncommon problem. There is no need for sleep clinics.' Ishaan made chortling sounds.

'Many babies are not wanting to sleep. You try to help him but the situation has become untenable for you. So what you have to do is simple. At bedtime tell the baby: "Baby, I love you, but I am sorry I can no longer rock you. Now you must sleep yourself because it is unsustainable for me otherwise." Then kiss him, say goodnight and leave.'

Goldman had essentially repeated exactly what Julio had been urging me to do for weeks, but from his lips it sounded as reasonable as it had sounded irresponsible from Julio's.

I reminded Goldman once again that Ishaan was only three months old. Wouldn't it be tantamount to cruelty to just let him cry? After all, despite all my interventions, the baby was not getting adequate sleep, which was the very reason I was at the doctor's office. 'Madame,' replied Goldman, as implacable as the Great Wall of China, 'what is cruel is to deprive him of the ability to sleep.'

That evening, as the clock struck seven, Julio and I sat grimly in the living room. Ishaan was dressed in the sweetest teddy-bear-smattered onesie, his sparse hair slicked back with the water from his recent bath. Julio turned to me. 'Go!' he ordered harshly, and I fled to the farthest corner of the house – the study, from where I had once upon a time filed newspaper reports.

After around five minutes I began to hear muffled crying of a pitch that splinters glass to smithereens. It was distant and distorted, yet felt as wretched as if it were smashing crockery inside my own head. I immediately left the study and went rushing back to the living room where Julio sat hunched, glaring at the muted TV set. Ishaan was screaming blue murder in his next-door bedroom. Julio pulled out a stopwatch. 'Two more minutes,' he said. We had decided to go in to check on the baby (but not pick him up) at five-minute intervals, gradually increasing the time between our visits.

I begged Julio to stop the torture. Let's just cradle him and bounce him around the house like usual. I won't complain any more, I promised. I begged. I cajoled. But Julio was unbending. He shooed me back into the study, this time with headphones to cover my ears.

I lay down on the study couch for a few minutes. The next thing I knew it was pitch black and terrifyingly silent. I swatted away the headphones that still enveloped my ears and stood up, disoriented in the darkness. As I stumbled towards a light switch a most unusual feeling overcame me: restfulness. I looked at my watch. It was 2 a.m. I had slept for almost seven hours straight.

Something between euphoria and disbelief bubbled within me. The maximum amount of unbroken sleep I'd managed in months was three hours. And then I felt a moment of blind panic. Something must have happened to the baby, which explained why it was all so quiet.

I ran towards Ishaan's bedroom, falling over a sleeping cat on the way. It was Tofu. She meowed in displeasure and flashed me an angry, green-eyed look. I ignored her and rushed on. I opened the door to Ishaan's bedroom, sweating with unease. And there he lay: my baby, sleeping in his cot, breathing rhythmically, eyes firmly shut, no squirming. Next door, Julio was snoring deeply, sprawled across our bed.

I went back to the living room and collapsed in wonder on an armchair. Both cats had woken by now and milled around my legs. I felt a surge of reserve affection in me and picked them up for a snuggle. The colic had perhaps been harder on Caramel and Tofu than anyone else. I could only imagine their complete bewilderment at having had their former lives as the cynosure of their parents' eyes disappear with the arrival of a crinkly skinned and perpetually wailing upstart.

As I sat there in the balm-like quiet I felt tears of relief prick my eyes as I paid mental obeisance to Dr Goldman, and Julio, for having insisted on this sleep 'training'.

The next morning Julio told me of a harrowing hour and a half in which he'd made repeated visits to the baby's room, reassuring him of love verbally, but refusing to pick him up. Ishaan had flailed and howled, but eventually cried himself to sleep. It sounded sad and barbaric. But the transformation in Ishaan that day was phenomenal. He was bright-eyed and relaxed. He giggled when we pretended to eat him up because he was just so sweet. I realized that much of his 'colic' had in fact just been exhaustion.

As the week progressed, the sleep 'training' got easier. By the end of ten days we were down to three to five minutes of fussing before bedtime, followed by hours of deep slumber. Ishaan still woke up for a bottle at some point in the middle of the night, but went promptly back to sleep again. It seemed preternatural. A month earlier I'd have had greater confidence in the idea that Caramel and Tofu could suddenly start speaking perfect English and cook us chicken soup for dinner, than that of my baby waking up only once at night.

By the end of January 2009, we were even able to contemplate a much put-off journey back to India, to introduce Ishaan to friends and family. We booked plane tickets and I began to research surviving long plane rides with a baby. 'Make sure to feed the baby on take-off and arrival so that his ears stay open,' friends posted on Facebook. 'Take a baby sling so you can walk up and down the aisles and still have your arms free,' another advised. 'You'll be just fine,' a third reassured. And astonishingly enough, I believed I would be.

My first brush with motherhood had been painful and ended with formula feeding and sleep training, both ideas that had been anathema to me when a baby had been an idea rather than a reality. But then the best parents always are those without any children.

A few weeks later we were out sitting on the vast green lawns of New Delhi's Gymkhana Club. Ishaan was propped up in his pram, looking around at all the family friends who sat sipping tea and snacking on finger foods. 'What a sweetie,' said one samosa-chomping auntie, clucking in his direction. 'What a peaceful little chap. Just like a little Buddha.'

4

CHOICE

2009–10, BEIJING–BRUSSELS

A clutter of boxes and bubble wrap, material portents of the impending move, stared at me accusingly. The Aunties Li and Mei swished by in blurs of stashing and lashing activity. After almost seven years in China, we were getting ready to move to Brussels, the famously dull and damp capital of Belgium. Julio was to take up a job in the trade directorate of the European Commission. And I had landed myself a new position as Europe correspondent for one of India's leading business newspapers.

But for the moment I was still plugging away at China stories at my desk in Beijing. It was April 2009, and I'd been back at work for a few months, ever since Ishaan turned four months old in age and Buddha-ish in temperament. But although during the height of Ishaan's 'colic' my greatest fantasies had revolved around a computer screen and me in solitary communion, now that I was back at the desk, I felt sluggish.

I was neither mentally nor physically akin to the deadline demon of China reporting I'd been for so many years. News of an earthquake did not see me hotfooting it to the airport clasping a granola-bar-filled backpack. The idea that someone at the newspaper headquarters in India might actually care enough to call and ask me to – shudder – *travel* to the affected location left me quite terrified.

No one called. No one ever had. When I had started work as a journalist in Beijing in 2002, I was only the second Indian correspondent covering China. My lone compatriot had been a rather timid gentleman in the employ of India's state-owned newswire, who had spent a decade living in Beijing without managing to learn a word of Chinese, and who rarely left his apartment. By the time 2009 rolled by, there were only two other Indian correspondents in town.

Reporting that entailed travel and translators remained for the most part the prerogative of Western foreign correspondents. That I'd learnt Chinese and wandered the length of the country in search of stories that had little or no direct connection to India (as opposed to: 'Indian minister visits Chinese Special Economic Zones', or 'Yoga becoming craze in China') was exceptional.

But four months post-baby I was acting distinctly state-owned news-wireish, rehashing press releases between researching baby milestones online. I felt Brutus-like. What a sellout I'd turned out to be. What had happened to my feminist principles? To my strongly held belief that motherhood did not affect, and should not be perceived as affecting, a woman's professionalism?

It took me years, and a second child, to figure out that in fact motherhood should affect a woman's approach to work, as a man's; that becoming parents changes us, and that this transformation is healthy and needs to be anticipated rather than brushed under the carpet under the guise of 'professionalism'; that change does not have to be deleterious, or that 'affect' doesn't necessarily equal 'harm'.

Parents, if they are at all involved in their new roles, will inevitably alter the manner in which they tackle their professional lives. They now have important competing priorities that require large investments of time. Their jobs cannot be their only focus, even if they can, and usually do, remain a substantial focus.

Before they have children the opportunity cost for most ambitious people in embracing workaholism entails less time to tweeze their nose hair, drink vodkas or exercise their cats. For parents working round the clock is to fail their children. This is an opportunity cost of a different magnitude.

The change in attitude towards 'work' that many parents develop involves a healthier perspective on professional life. Neither the world nor one's professional standing will end if one needs a day off to take a sick child to the doctor. Yet, in most professional contexts, attempting any kind of genuine work–life balance is seen as unprofessional, and is often detrimental to both career and peace of mind. 'Of course I can stay in the office till 10 p.m.,' one must always acquiesce. 'What? My two-year-old? Oh, that's not a problem. He can barely talk.'

However, despite all the gains of feminism, in most professions men who become fathers continue to act like they have not been changed by parenthood. And women who acknowledge this change are punished for it. They are usually compelled to either give up their professional lives (or at least any hope of serious ambition), or to become complicit in the system, in the manner of a majority of men, and consequently to neglect their children.[1]

The construction and perpetuation of this false dichotomy between the personal and professional, between parents and professionals, is amongst the worst sins of contemporary work culture.

The continuing, arguably defining, angst that women of my generation exhaust themselves pondering is that tired yet stubborn query: can women have it all?

Of course no one can have it all; life is about compromises and trade-offs for everyone. But no one can even have adequate portions of a wide range of human experiences and achievements if their professional success and identity entail working all the time.

Men, stuck in this rut, certainly don't have it all either. Children don't have it all if they are faced with the choice of either absent or thwarted parents. Even capitalism isn't having it all given that talented and capable women are keeping away from the workforce simply because they have children.

I was determined to stay in the workforce, which was one of the reasons I'd accepted the new job in Brussels even though it entailed a pay cut. Europe was a harder sell to an Indian audience than China, a country that India was pathologically obsessed with.

But there was also another reason I hadn't demurred when confronted with the prospect of lower pay: I knew that my commitment to the job (which was high) would have competition vis-á-vis my commitments to Ishaan. Earning less than I had before becoming a mother helped assuage imagined future guilt at prioritizing my child over a story. As it transpired, that situation arose so rarely as to be insignificant, but the fear of an employer equating reasonable pay with unfettered commitment never went away in all the subsequent years.

Baby milestones marked the months to our departure for Brussels. Ishaan rolled over. He sat up. He sprouted two teeth. And then, one more. He drank from a sippy cup. He ate puréed carrots and made a mess on the kitchen floor.

Before we knew it, Julio, Ishaan, Caramel, Tofu and I were in Brussels. It was springtime and the streets were lined with cherry blossoms in bloom. Glossy wood pigeons cooed from their branches. The weather was balmy; sunny without any real heat. We walked everywhere.

We based ourselves near Schuman, the area that was home to the majority of the European Union's offices, and began our search for a home. The clean air, vast green parks, stroller-friendly pavements and statuesque houses made for a startling, and happy, change from Beijing's smog, phlegm-dotted walkways and incessant construction.

(It wasn't long before this honeymoon was over and Brussels' skies returned to their crepuscular norm, the statuesque fin-de-siècle houses revealed themselves to have plumbing problems even as every plumber in the city had gone off on a two-month-long vacation, and the expense of everything from a haircut to a pair of shoes had us in a constant state of near cardiac arrest. But this was in the future.)

The icing on the cake in those early days in Brussels was Ishaan. He had morphed into the 'ideal baby', the kind that slept in his stroller while I read a book and sipped a drink at a neighbourhood coffee shop. It was quite a metamorphosis from the endless nights I'd spent bouncing him up and down, '*Buffalo Soldier*' blaring in the background, wondering what nefarious deeds I had done in my past life to deserve such knee-breaking karma.

We managed to find a home to rent within a week's time and then set about buying washing machines and vacuum cleaners, and organizing Internet and phone connections. By week three I had begun to tire of playing 'house'. By week four, pushing Ishaan endlessly up and down the same warren of streets, tree-lined and phlegm-free though they may have been, began to drive me to five cups of coffee a day.

The bald fact was that I really did not enjoy spending all day with my baby, even now, when I had less of an excuse given his post-colic avatar. Sitting for hour after hour in a largely unfurnished home, entertaining a seven-month-old, felt like the experiential equivalent of nails scraping a wall.

I played him music, I rattled toys, I tried to force him to spend at least half an excruciating hour on his tummy (the latest baby advice from the 'experts', supposedly helpful in strengthening the muscles needed to crawl), I puréed foods, I carefully brushed all four of his teeth after every meal, I got down on the play mat and batted at dangly things with him. I felt my mind slowly and steadily calcify.

It was slightly better outdoors. So I spent a lot of hours in public playgrounds, which were a plentiful and well-maintained feature of the city's parks. But the other moms spooked me with their lonely eyes and 'how old is he, what a cutie' conversation. Perhaps this was only because they mirrored me. And I did not like what the mirror revealed.

I yearned for the time and mental space to write my book (I was by now working on my first novel), to begin reporting, to walk about the city on my own (flânerie was not quite the same with a stroller glued to your palms), and to learn French. In short, I yearned for a nanny.

My greatest dread about moving to Europe had entailed childcare. I had been brought up in India, in an upper-middle-class family, where nannies were considered more important than, and were almost as ubiquitous as, furniture in the house. Sending a baby to a crèche or day-care centre, as was the norm in Brussels, felt somewhat cruel. I was determined to wait until Ishaan was at least a year old. Besides, there were long waiting lists for the best day-care centres and the European Commission's crèche gave preference to single moms and families where both parents worked for the Commission. We were told it might take a year before we got a place.

I was also wholly incompetent at housework. I couldn't cook. I couldn't iron with any skill. I found washing machines scary. I was an elite-in-a-developing-country kind of brat. And I was fast realizing that I'd rather go bungee jumping than commit to being a stay-at-home mom. In any case, tending house had never been part of my plan. I had a new job to start. Although the newspaper had told me to take my time settling in (a reflection, perhaps, of just how important 'Europe' was to the Indian media), I couldn't delay forever.

The nanny 'problem' was essentially one of expense. We could afford one only if I all but handed over my salary to her. So, did it make sense for me to work only in order to be able to pay someone else to look after my child? Hell, yes! For me, it was a no-brainer.

People who thought this question was even worth raising were obviously those who either did not adore their jobs and/or did not find looking after their own babies as dull as I did. This was probably a capacious category of humans. Not many people like their jobs. And many mothers appear to love looking after their little angels all day.

The other factor that helped me answer that question so emphatically in the affirmative was that covering Europe for a newspaper whose readers didn't particularly care about the subject resulted in a large degree of work flexibility.

On most days I had to file before 4 p.m. (given the time difference with India), which meant I was almost always able to give Ishaan dinner and a bath before tucking him in for the night. Since there was only rarely any breaking news from the continent that interested Indians, I was able to focus on feature writing, which entails a slower pace than hard news. My boss was thousands of kilometres away and I had no colleagues to judge how much office time I was putting in.

It was around this time that a much loved cousin, who'd had her first baby a few months after Ishaan was born, announced that she had decided not to return to work. My cousin was a successful corporate lawyer, educated in some of the best universities in the world. She had always been a driven individual.

While she was still pregnant she'd asked me what I thought was the minimum possible time before she could return to work post-partum. 'Four months,' I'd ventured cautiously, an answer she'd immediately dismissed with a 'that's too long'. I remember thinking how difficult it was to explain just how time consuming an infant was, to someone who didn't have one yet. I'd considered trying to describe it to her. Then, I'd thought better of it. Why discourage her? Perhaps her child would be different. Or perhaps she would react differently to having a child. I'd held my tongue and changed the subject

That only a few months on my cousin had categorically renounced all intentions of ever returning to work left me gobsmacked and vaguely anxious. I simply couldn't square that decision with the person I knew her to be. She visited me a while later in Brussels, when her daughter was a year old. She was passing through the Belgian capital en route to India, on her way back from a holiday in the United States.

I found the idea of travelling alone with Ishaan on a different continent about as appetizing as a platter of sea slugs and had been amazed that my cousin had undertaken such an enterprise. I'd also felt a tad disheartened at her obviously superior competence at motherhood.

But when my cousin showed up she was exhausted and weepy from the long journey. She had not morphed into some kind of ninja mom who never tired of looking after her perfect child. She was in fact reassuringly schizophrenic and overwhelmed. One moment she smiled at her daughter in pure joy. The next moment she was hissing that babies sucked the lifeblood out of you. I wanted to high-five her in solidarity. Yet I also had to ask what on earth had possessed her to quit her high-powered, high-paying job?

My cousin sighed. She'd obviously been explaining herself for a while now. Given her family background it had been almost as difficult for her to decide to stay at home, as it would be for a woman with a very traditional upbringing to decide to work outside the house. Both decisions involved defying expectations, ignoring disapproval and battling stigma.

Even though I'd said little, I had felt let down by my cousin and I had disapproved of her decision. I knew it was politically correct to believe that every woman should have the right to choose what was best for her, but deep down in my soul, where it was so dark that political correctness was unable to make itself seen, I believed that a woman who chose to spend all day wiping snot and planning 'healthy snacks' was wasting her education and slapping feminism in the face. She was perpetuating patriarchy and doing no one, including her children, any favours.

Listening to my cousin's explanation was therefore an uncomfortable experience. Nothing she said was revolutionary. I had heard and read similar stories before. Coming from someone I knew and loved, however, the narrative gained a force that compelled me to emphathize.

My cousin explained that she had in fact returned to work when her daughter was around six months old and had immediately found herself in an impossible position. The hours she had to put in at her firm were brutal. At home she was unable to find reliable childcare. Her husband was also a lawyer with equally long, if not longer, hours. There was no point in having had a baby if she never got to spend time with her, and there was also no point in having a job if she spent most of her time worrying about her baby and resenting her work. It was the classic conundrum that women in corporate settings face.

My immediate response was one that had already been put to her on more occasions than she cared to remember. Why don't you just dial it down, I suggested. Go part-time for a while, until your daughter is older?

My cousin replied that it would make her deeply frustrated to sit around doing bits and bobs of work, while less competent male colleagues outstripped her in pay, and scaled the heights of a corporate ladder that she would be left merely guarding her space on.

But what about the enjoyment that she would get from her work, I queried. Didn't that have a value over and beyond a pay cheque or promotion? Not really, she replied. It turned out that my cousin didn't love her job for her job's sake. She enjoyed it for the financial compensation and the professional prestige; for the sense of achievement that the ladder-climbing engendered. But she did not feel this was the kind of job where it was worthwhile, or enjoyable, to just stand still.

As we sat talking late into the afternoon I found myself understanding her choice. I was also thankful for her, and me, that we had choices to make, despite being Satre-fully aware of the weight of having only ourselves to blame for the consequences of those choices.

These choices depend on our personalities, on the temperaments of our babies, on the flexibility of our employers, and the parameters according to which success happens to be measured in our professions. They also depend on our financial status, on the attitudes of our spouses, and on whether or not our own mothers had worked.[2] Any choice is obviously the outcome of a delicate web of circumstances, a fact that should in theory militate against prescriptive attitudes and harsh judgements. So why are the 'mommy wars', in which stay-at-home moms square off against working mothers, so infamously vitriolic?

Perhaps because the decision to work outside the home, or to raise kids full-time, speaks loudly on behalf of the decision maker, regarding her (and occasionally his) assumptions about gender, finance and marriage. This 'choice' is such an intimate and often tortured (for there are inevitably painful trade-offs involved) statement of one's identity that it makes it difficult for someone who chooses one way to empathize with someone who has arrived at a different decision. Sometimes there is an underlying fear that the other choice is in fact the better one. Sometimes there is anger at having been forced to make a choice at all, given the unacceptability of the 'choice'.

Talking with my cousin helped me appreciate her decision. It was clear why she, and other women in positions similar to her, elected to stay at home given their life and work circumstances. But it also left me with the conviction that these circumstances needed to change. No parent can be expected to bring up a child satisfactorily if their work environment is wilfully blind to the fact of their parenthood.

This was why although 'choice' is an important part of empowerment, I found 'choice feminism', or the idea that any choice a woman makes is a feminist one simply because it is chosen, quite absurd. In an especially memorable episode of the TV series *Sex and the City*, the character of Charlotte justifies her decision to stop working by repeatedly shouting down the phone, 'I choose my choice.' But, feminism is not just about choice. It is about change.

While I agree that women should have the right to decide what is best for them, exclusively focusing on choice can distract from the limited range of those choices.

One of the more choice examples of 'choice feminism' was the 2015 video featuring Indian movie actress, Deepika Padukone, that went viral on social media.[3] The video had Ms Padukone performing a voice-over to a montage of several 'empowered'-looking women, with statements such as:

'To be a size zero or size fifteen ... My choice.'

'To have sex before marriage, to have sex outside of marriage ... My choice.'

'My choice: to have your baby or not.'

The idea that choosing to have a baby does not involve a partner, that sex outside marriage is a lifestyle choice that can't be questioned, and that women simply choose their body size, is enough for anyone to immediately want to banish 'choice' from the human lexicon.

Feminism is a political stance not just a lifestyle. If choice becomes the yardstick by which to determine gender justice, deep structural change becomes a casualty. An emphasis on choice responds to available options rather than highlighting the need to widen those options. Equal pay, paternity leave, political representation, workplace flexibility – these are not choices that exist for most people. But they should.

My conversation with my cousin helped slap me down a notch or two on the pride/arrogance scale. I had been feeling quite pleased with myself for 'having it all'. I affected humility and talked about how exhausted I was when people complimented me for 'doing so much' – writing an entire book, while reporting on a new subject, all with a baby who couldn't even walk yet. But when someone gushingly asked how I managed to accomplish it all, in reality it would set me smugly aglow inside.

In fact, my seemingly perfect work–life balance had less to do with the Herculean 'leaning-in'[4] on my part, than with incredible good fortune and helpful circumstances. I only had one child (two, as I was to find out, adds a whole new layer of complexity), a spouse who earned well (which allowed me to accept a pay cut) and was supportive of my career, a job that I really enjoyed, a flexible schedule that had me working from home for the most part, a mother who was an incredible role model for any working mom, and last but not at all the least, a nanny. I had genuine choices which made me, more than anything else, lucky.

In Brussels nothing preoccupied me more than childcare. Until Ishaan found a place at the European Commission crèche I depended on a number of babysitters. Every time one of them quit, or fell sick, or had boyfriend issues and didn't show for work, I initially felt as though the floor had given way under me. Instead of certainty there was confusion. There was apologizing and reorganizing. There were times when appointments got missed and writing schedules fell off the wagon, for a day or two.

But, remarkably, despite the feeling of black hopelessness that inevitably followed a childcare disruption, no serious work consequence resulted. Julio stepped in if it was urgent. On occasion I managed to meet article deadlines by writing even as Ishaan played noisily next to my desk. And by the time he was two years old, we had found a place for him at the European Commission's crèche, which removed our nanny dependency for the most part.

My career chugged along. *Smoke and Mirrors* won a literary award. My novel, *Chinese Whiskers*, was written and published in several countries. And I began to report on the intricacies of the European Union. Many of my days were spent shuttling between the offices of the European Commission and the Indian embassy in Brussels.

I made short trips to various Belgian cities like Antwerp, where I profiled Gujarati diamond merchants from India who had managed to oust orthodox Jews as the doyens of the business. I visited power generation equipment makers in Mechelen, gherkin bottlers in Aalst and pharmaceutical companies in Beerse. My longest trip away from the family was in December 2009 when I spent ten cold days in Copenhagen, covering the United Nations' Climate Change conference.

I had developed an odd relationship with travel. Before I became a mother I'd hated plane travel for all the usual reasons: the terrible food, the cramped spaces, the inescapable delays and the interminable security queues. After having children, however, long plane trips became an imagined refuge, where I could read entire novels uninterrupted or just allow myself to succumb to the unplanned pleasures of daydreaming.

Unfortunately, this imagined utopia rarely came to pass. My daydreams inevitably morphed into nightmares about instructions I'd forgotten to give the nanny, or dreadful playground accidents that could see Ishaan maimed for life. And instead of reading long, intellectually challenging novels, I often found myself sneaking online to read about development milestones that Ishaan should have been hitting, but was not. Other babies were walking by the time they were nine months old, while Ishaan had only just started to crawl as his first birthday came around. Even worse, other babies crawled with immaculate posture and advanced coordination, but Ishaan had developed a lopsided crab-like shuffle that was ungainly even to a mother's biased eyes.

But my greatest fantasy around travel had to do with the thought of sleep. I always hoped that a sealed-off hotel room far from any children waking up in the middle of the night complaining of nightmares/thirst/tummy ache, or desirous of nocturnal playing/singing/hunting for stuffed toys, would automatically equate peaceful slumber. Unhappily, I found that my post-partum insomnia travelled with me. And no matter if I was in Copenhagen or New York with ne'er a child in sight, I slept poorly, all the more aggravated for having no excuse for my disturbed nights.

Exhaustion was therefore probably the single greatest difference between life *before* and *after* Baby for me. And this despite the fact that unlike the vast majority of women I had a nanny to help out and a job that required little physical labour.

I had dinner with a British friend, a mom of three boys, in Brussels one evening when she quipped about how she found it amusing to recall ever having complained of tiredness before she'd become a mother. 'Do you remember complaining how *tired* you were before you had a child?' I'd found myself laughing so hard

I'd had to put down my drink from fear of spilling it, even though it wasn't a very funny joke. But perhaps that was precisely why I'd laughed so much.

By the time Ishaan was eighteen months old, he was well on the path to Nobel laureateship. He could correctly identify all twenty-six letters of the English alphabet and could point to examples of the human male while enunciating 'man', most clearly. (Calling out 'man' after random men was admittedly a tad rude, but better than Ishaan's first attempts at naming which had him excitedly shouting 'Papa' at every man we encountered.)

He was also very musical and enjoyed the Build Your Baby's Brain CDs we conscientiously played him that featured specially chosen parts from various Mozart symphonies and concertos. Bursting with pride at Ishaan's genius, I must have been insufferable to be around.

I remember having a German friend who had a daughter, Kathy, only a few weeks younger than Ishaan, over for tea. At some point as we sipped our English Breakfast I innocuously remarked how lovely it was that kids seemed to have such a natural love of classical music. 'Take, Ishaan,' I'd continued breezily, 'he's only able to sleep after humming the entire overture of '*The Marriage of Figaro*'.

This was actually true. Ishaan had taken to da da-ing out parts of the opera after I'd tucked him in for bed. But the effect of this anecdote on my friend was cruel. She'd looked crestfallen and mumbled something about her daughter only being familiar with nursery rhymes.

My casual remark had at once signalled to her that my son was more 'advanced' than her daughter, and that I was a better mother. I hadn't made the remark in malice and had regretted the words as soon as they'd left my mouth. After all I was no stranger to the intense and wholly unreasonable jealousy that another child's 'accomplishments' could provoke in a mother's breast.

There was, for instance, a nine-month-old I had once bumped into at the Parc du Cinquantenaire, a lush expanse of green near our home, who was actually wobbling around on his two feet *walking,* while Ishaan was still only getting about with his ungainly crab crawl despite being three months older. I had felt a stinging sensation of misery in my heart as the athletic baby had casually chucked a ball towards the prostrate Ishaan (and with much better aim than Ishaan could have managed too).

But my German friend should not have been too crestfallen, despite my boasting. Ishaan might have been a Mozart aficionado while Kathy preferred 'Three Blind Mice', but my little maestro was also fast transforming into a 'Terrible Two' personified: obstinate, tantrum-prone, defiant and, frankly, bratty. Meltdowns were Ishaan's de facto response to pretty much all of life. When he didn't get his banana. When he did get his banana. When I asked him not to play with kitchen knives. When I asked him not to stick his fingers in electrical sockets. When I suggested he take a nap. And when he was tired.

His natural reaction to every proposal was to oppose, and to every instruction, to defy. This was worse than colic. It was after all much more reasonable to ascribe blame for a toddler's bad behaviour to his parents than it was to blame them for an infant's inexplicable crying.

I'd never really liked young children. They'd always seemed to drool and run amok far too much for my liking. Indian children were amongst the worst offenders: shrieking on planes, refusing to sit quietly in restaurants, demanding chocolates from overly indulgent parents. In contrast, children in Europe seemed better mannered.

In Brussels, I regularly encountered smartly dressed mothers with three children, all under the age of five, eating together in cafes. Remarkably, they seemed to get through these meals without developing hypertension. I noticed ten-month-olds gummily self-feeding healthy finger foods like avocado chunks from the specially prepared snack boxes that these mothers carried about with them. Older toddlers might be spotted having minor tantrums, but these were mild and usually consisted of some short-lived pouting and whining rather than the 'goat in imminent danger of being slaughtered' shrieks that were Ishaan's particular talent.

If, as was sometimes claimed, colic did not exist in the developing world, I sometimes felt that brats did not exist in Europe.

Some of these divergences were obviously rooted in differential attitudes, and circumstances, related to child raising. In India, for example, sugar was not equated with Satan, as it had come to be in the West. Parents regularly fed their kids makkhan (butter), roti (wheat bread), cheeni (sugar), while slurping back cups of chai sweetened with tablespoons of sugar themselves.

Children in India, as in China, also routinely slept with parents, and many were spoon-fed for far later than their toddling counterparts in Europe. While a few of these practices, notably the sugar, were not the best long-term choices to be made, others did the kids little harm and probably brought them greater happiness.

The fact was that for most (middle-class) Indian families, nannies and grandparents were a taken-for-granted part of the childcare scene, which afforded parents, mothers in particular, the luxury of greater indulgence towards their little ones. The availability of more adult hands to help out with kids meant that there was less urgency in pushing children to be independent. Babies often slept with grandmothers or ayahs, giving mothers the chance to sleep at night and therefore to eliminate the need for 'sleep training'. Kids were commonly hand-fed by members of the extended family, or by hired help, until they naturally began to eat by themselves.

Westerners could be remarkably judgemental of some of these practices. In China, for example, it was standard for those who could afford it, to hire a *yue-sao* or doula to help new mothers with everything from breastfeeding to nutritious diets and baths.

At one of the childbirth classes I had attended in Beijing, a young Chinese woman, who was a month or so post-partum and an alumna of the group herself, dropped in to talk about her experience of giving birth at the hospital. Once she was done expounding on episiotomies and other vaginal niceties, the expectant mothers (all foreigners) began to press her about life with a baby. 'Are you simply exhausted?' asked one heavily pregnant French lady, her eyes round with excited sympathy. 'Not really,' the Chinese woman replied with a smile. 'My yue-sao sleeps with the baby and gives her the night bottles, so I can get some rest.'

The room exploded in consternation. 'You mean you don't sleep with your baby?' 'You mean you don't feed your baby yourself?' The questions were thick with recrimination. The young mother felt the barbs keenly. Her facial expression alternated between guilt and bewilderment as she repeatedly stressed that the milk in the bottles that the yue-sao was giving the baby contained breast milk. 'It's my milk, from here,' she said, touching her bosom. 'I pump in the day. I pump.' But her explanations only met with a huffy silence.

In Europe, mothers rarely experience the privilege of hired help, or even the assistance of extended families. This places enormous burdens on mothers (while leaving them somewhat judgemental of those cultures where the job of child rearing is shared. But it also means that European kids are more self-sufficient. A child who does not sleep, eat or dress by herself/himself, is understandably unacceptable to a mother already overwhelmed by responsibilities at home and in the professional world.

Day care is another reason that children in Europe are less spoilt than in many other parts of the world.[5] Upon finding themselves only one amongst scores of kids vying for the attention of a couple of beleaguered teachers, most children learn to look after their own basic needs quite early on.

I was determined that Ishaan would overcome his genetic heritage and be *well behaved* in true European style. The formula for this transcendence had seemed obvious: zero indulgence, clear boundary setting, strict policing of said borders, a refusal to 'baby' the child, and packing him off to crèche once this was feasible.

But trying to ensure that Ishaan fed himself, put on his own shoes, and tidied up his own toys turned out to be a physically painful experience. It took inhuman levels of self-control to stop myself from screaming when, despite hours of showing him how to eat yoghurt with a spoon, he still managed to smear it all over his freshly washed hair while simultaneously flinging a good-sized dollop at my laptop computer halfway across the room. Unfortunately, I was, as most mothers are, human. And so I did scream on occasion. Which only served to trigger a toddler tantrum. And in turn led to my suffering miserable bouts of guilt and self-recrimination.

Eventually, and inevitably, I took to Google to try and understand what was going on with Ishaan's meltdowns. And as usual, I was left muddled and remorseful: the standard effect of so much parenting advice.

On the one hand, I came away convinced that my toddler was suffering from the sinister, but accurately descriptive, 'oppositional defiant disorder'. The symptoms of this horrible condition fitted Ishaan to a T: 'negativity, defiance, disobedience'.[6]

But on the other hand I read articles entitled 'The gift of the strong-willed child'[7] and the like, which stressed that 'strong-willed' children were gifts from God and would likely grow up to be confident, decisive leaders. I needed to learn to appreciate my child for who he was and not for what I wanted him to be. I needed to have a positive attitude and relabel my child from 'stubborn' to 'persistent', and from 'defiant' to 'spirited'. I needed to find ways to work *with* him, rather than in opposition to him. I had to 'tame' *myself,* rather than trying to tame him.

There were, however, some basic tenets emphasized in every school of thought: parents needed to set clear boundaries, be consistent in enforcing these and stay calm when dealing with tantrums. I failed on all three counts quite regularly.

Ishaan would beg to take a toy along with him for the ride to school. Believing that enlightened parenting lay in providing him the opportunity to find entertainment in his natural environment, rather than in a noisy, plastic toy, I would say no. He would cry and rage in response. Finally, after fifteen minutes of trying to block out the screeching while failing to stuff my son's flailing body into a coat and shoes, I'd often cave in.

I comforted myself with the thought that I hadn't allowed him to play with kitchen knives. Yet.

But much parenting advice also suggested, 'picking one's battles'. The idea was to limit saying 'no' to the child to the minimum. 'No' to situations in which they would endanger themselves and 'yes' to all other non-critical desires.

And thus began the toothbrush reign of terror. One evening as I was brushing my teeth, Ishaan, who was splashing about in shallow water in the bathtub, pointed to my toothbrush and stated 'want', in his signature unvarnished manner. I smiled indulgently, and gently explained that he couldn't have my toothbrush and handed him his own instead. He immediately threw his own toothbrush aside with a scream, as if I had handed him a piece of burning coal. The screaming did not stop. With toothpaste foam pouring out of my mouth I tried to reason with him; to explain the mechanics of oral cavity bacteria and the nefarious effects of their transfer. It was of no use.

'Pick your battles', I suddenly remembered and with a sigh, in equal parts of relief and defeat, I washed out my brush and handed it to my son. He immediately began to chew on it happily; the stream of tears running down his cheeks magically drying up. But over the next several weeks it became impossible for Julio or me to brush our teeth in view of Ishaan. The instant he saw us trying to practise any kind of dental hygiene, he would demand our brushes.

Brushing the teeth became a highly charged clandestine activity. We took to buying decoy toothbrushes. We hid our 'real' ones and only put the dummies out on display, in the hope that we could fob off fakes on the boy. Sometimes it worked. At other times there was more tantrum

In desperation I turned to that time-tested miracle maker and colic banisher, Harvey Karp. An order on Amazon and few days' wait later, it arrived in the post: *The Happiest Toddler on the Block: How to Eliminate Tantrums and Raise a Patient, Respectful, and Cooperative One to Four-Year-Old.* I read Karp's book cover to cover in one sitting, filled with manic hope that an end to tantrums was nigh.

His toddler theory, in essence, is that young children are cavemen. Like their Neanderthal ancestors, toddlers are stubborn, opinionated and lacking in complex vocabulary. They bite, spit and grunt. They react physically when angry. They are sloppy eaters, hate to wait in line, and are negative, distractable and impatient.

An epiphany dawned. Ishaan was not an 'Indian baby', he was just an Australopithecus. According to Karp, toddlers actually find it upsetting when their demands, which to them feel like visceral needs, are met with calm and logic. They feel, he theorized, as though their feelings are not getting across. What is required, therefore, is for the adult to mirror the little caveman's desire in tone and content, so that the child understands that he is being understood, a process that helps diffuse tantrums in the offing.

What Karp advises is for parents to get down on their knees and loudly repeat the crux of what the tantrumming child is trying to communicate, back at them. So, for example, were Ishaan to begin to scream because he wanted my toothbrush, I needed to bring my face close to his and with exaggerated accompanying hand movements shout back: 'You want? You want this? Ishaan wants Mama's toothbrush? You want it now?' At this point, according to Karp's methodology, Ishaan would magically stop crying, which would be the precise moment to finally introduce firm logic in the way of a 'I know you want it, but this is not yours. Here, have another toothbrush instead.'

I spent the next several months constantly shouting, 'YOU WANT SNACK/RAT POSION/GARBAGE/SHAMPOO,' etc., back at Ishaan, sometimes in public. Neighbours began avoiding me. But I didn't care, because it worked. Every time I tried 'toddler-ese', as Karp called this staccato, overwrought form of communicating, Ishaan would startle into silence at the sight of his crazy cavewoman mom rotating her arms around like windmills, while screaming, 'THIS IS MINE. THIS IS ISHAAN'S. NO GIVE YOU, MAMA.'

As with colic, Karp's techniques proved to be useful coping mechanisms, although they did not 'solve' the problem. Ishaan continued to have meltdowns and although toddler-ese often helped nip one in the bud, there were other times that nothing worked. Except time. With children it almost always comes down to time.

Regardless of whether the issue is potty training, or sleep, or a tendency towards tantrums, eventually, with time, the most extreme aspects of these problems wane. The adage, 'this too shall pass', is a staple of parenting community websites. And with good reason. Unfortunately, the 'passing' often takes inordinately long. In years to come I would sometimes joke with Ishaan how at least two mountains had formed somewhere in the world in the time it took him to finish up his dinner and put away his dishes.

Moreover, time and parenting form a non-linear equation. With every problem solved, another takes its place.

I remember desperately asking assorted other mothers when it would all get easier. They would look at me kindly and string me along. 'Oh, the first month is tough, but then you get used to it,' one friend had said while I was still pregnant. 'By the time they're six months old, and on solids, you'll find it easier,' another opined a few months later. 'It gets so much better once they're walking,' I was told next. This was followed by, 'By the time they start talking, you'll find it all falls into place.' And then, 'They start becoming more reasonable at around four years old.' The ball just kept being kicked down the line. Until the grandmothers laughed about how 'you'll be worrying even when they're thirty.'

And in the meantime I continued to make a real hash of mothering. Far from being a constant and patient role model, I was short-tempered and irritated. Children do hold up a mirror to you. And the manner in which I reacted to many of the challenges that parenting Ishaan provoked, did not reveal a very flattering picture in that mirror. Here I was blaming Ishaan for being volatile, obstinate, and quick to anger, while I acted pretty much in the same way.

I had read somewhere that becoming a mother is to take up a gauntlet. It is an opportunity to introspect and become the person you would like to be, rather than continue as the snarky, impatient and stressed person you probably are. I failed the test. I remained resolutely irritable.

I didn't even cook. All I could do was put feta cheese cubes and olives into a snack box for Ishaan to take with him to the day-care centre every day. Actually, feta and olives were a pretty good snack for a two-year-old, right? I remember congratulating myself on the one aspect of my parenting skills that was above reproach: Ishaan had a wide-ranging palate and liked to eat all kinds of interesting foods. This was obviously testament to at least some of my de-bratifying strategy having worked. It comforted me. That is until I had a second child who ate nothing but bananas and raisins for virtually his entire pre-school life. But it was a nice thought while it lasted.

5

RINSE AND REPEAT

2010–11, BRUSSELS

I remember looking up from the finished manuscript of my novel, *Chinese Whiskers*, one afternoon, and glimpsing Ishaan playing in our back garden. He had recently turned two just as the weather had turned cold, the passing of another season marking his inexorable march out of toddlerdom. His cheeks were still puffy with baby fat, but a leaner jaw was beginning to show itself when he tilted his face at certain angles.

Ishaan was lining up his collection of assorted diggers and cement mixers with great concentration and sending up puffs of silky breath into the chilly air as he worked. All of a sudden, I felt this wave of love so strong it punched me in the face. I was felled by this emotion; floored by it. I wanted to sink my fingers into his tiny, yielding, body and inhale him. I wanted to mix him up with yoghurt and honey and make a Popsicle out of him. What was this love that consumed me, and indeed, provoked this urge to consume him? Where between all the sleepless nights and toothbrush tantrums had it found the space to sneak up and accost me like this?

The answer was opaque. There was no one moment when I abruptly realized the body ache with which I loved this child. I had spent more time feeling tormented, resentful, guilty and tired than delirious with joy these last two years. And yet the delirium had infected me despite, or was it because of, the tedium and routine! In the relentless everyday motions of brushing teeth, soothing fears, reading books, dancing, cleaning diapers, laughing, shouting, getting dressed, undressed, clipping nails and kicking balls, this love grew up and bit me. It often hid behind clouds of stress and exasperation, but it would unexpectedly peek out from behind these as well, as bright and warming as the morning sun.

I recalled many conversations I'd had with friends who were mothers, before I had Ishaan. With dark shadows under their eyes they'd recount a litany of torture that their infants were inflicting on them. But invariably, they would end with wan smiles and a weak 'But it's really worth it'. Nothing they had just said justified that conclusion and yet, it was the inevitable dénouement of these conversations. That afternoon I looked out at Ishaan in the garden and felt the irrational truth of those words.

Julio happened to pick that particular evening to broach the question of a second child. Until then the very idea of a number two had me quivering like a convulsive jellyfish. There were few things I knew with the certainty that I did not want to endure *again*, like colic, breastfeeding and sleep training. But Julio made the tentative suggestion only hours after I'd been buoyed up on that wave of maternal love that somehow anaesthetized the past. It had been a tough journey, but to quote all my mom friends, 'it had been worth it'.

I acquiesced.

And so sometime later I found myself staring at another double purple line on a stick I had just peed on. That evening, when I told

Julio, he gathered me up in his arms and looked radiant. I was happy too, but also a tad stricken, unable to shake the feeling of having jumped off a cliff, setting in motion a vertiginous chain of events that I would now be powerless to reverse.

Julio was quick to assuage my fears. Perhaps now we would have the little girl that we'd picked out a name for the last time round. Perhaps this time the pregnancy would not be accompanied by untamed vomiting. And perhaps this baby would not be 'colicky', and sleep with natural ease. As for breastfeeding, he continued, it was entirely up to me. Julio promised he would not interfere in decisions pertaining to lactation again.

I dared to allow myself to hope. After all, there seemed to be consensus on how second children were easier. I was one myself, and my mother had always claimed that she hadn't even noticed me growing up. Parents were less anxious when it came to second kids. They were more confident of their parenting skills and had already accepted the transformations that parenthood had wrought in their lives. The best part, I was universally assured, was how the kids would begin to play with each other, keeping themselves out of their parents' hair. It would be a cinch, apparently.

But then, week six of the pregnancy rolled around and, once again, I began a two-month-long embrace of the toilet bowl. The vomiting kicked off while I was on a trip investigating renewable energy projects in Austria. I continued, over the next few weeks, throwing up in various picturesque European locales, including Lisbon, where a big NATO (North Atlantic Treaty Organization) summit was taking place, and Liechtenstein, a tiny Alpine kingdom whose prince was about to travel to India on an official visit. And so it happened that the first, and only, time I saw President Barack Obama in person, at the NATO press conference, I had to leave immediately, handkerchief pushed against my mouth to hold back the malodorous regurgitation of what had been my breakfast. Ditto, His Serene Highness, Prince Alois, at his castle in the Liechtenstein capital of Vaduz.

Once again I felt apologetic when informing my employers of my pregnancy. I imagined them thinking, even as they smiled in put-on delight at my 'good news', about the extra expense my maternity would entail for them.

There were bottom lines involved at a time when the newspaper industry was facing tough challenges. India's economy was in a slump following several years of high growth, and advertising revenue was drying up. I was aware of a large number of lay-offs in the industry back home. I had been hired against the tide, given that more newspapers were closing foreign bureaus rather than opening them. And now, less than two years into the assignment, I would be less reliably available than 'normal', for several months, if not longer.

For the second time, I felt sabotaged by biology. I abhorred descriptions of women as the 'weaker sex', and yet I was weakened by the unending nausea. And this time I knew that pregnancy was only the short and easy warm-up act for the months that would follow the actual birth.

I doubled my efforts at work. I fought the nausea even when whimpering with exhaustion. I travelled, interviewed, and filed stories non-stop, fuelled by the anxiety of the potential toll that my pregnancy might take on my job. I had negotiated three months' paid maternity leave while on a quick trip to India. That particular discussion had been excruciatingly embarrassing for me. Asking for three months' pay for no (newspaper-related) work had felt like a big, and underserved, ask. I'd been ridiculously grateful when my editor had agreed without a fuss.

It was only much later, after I came across 'The Confidence Gap', a 2014 article by journalists Katty Kay and Claire Shipman in *The Atlantic* magazine,[1] when I first considered that perhaps something else had also been in play during the months I'd wrestled with pregnancy-related professional guilt: my gender. It is possible that I would have felt none, or much less, of the confounding complex of apology, anxiety and gratitude for my three months of maternity leave had I been a man.

What spoke to me in the article was how studies have consistently shown men to have a greater self-worth, professionally, than women. The authors referenced a number of research projects, which conclude that while men and women do not differ on average when it comes to their performance in the workplace, men consistently overestimate their abilities and performance, and women underestimate both.

The article mentions a study by Hewlett-Packard where a review of personnel records found that women tended to apply for a promotion only if they believed themselves to meet 100 per cent of the qualifications listed for the job. Men, however, jumped to apply even when they thought they could meet some 60 per cent of the job requirements. The authors' conclusion was that women feel confident only when they are perfect, or nearly so.

I was put in mind of countless discussions I'd had with Julio over the years. He was always brimming with ideas and possibilities: moving to China, writing books, applying for jobs. I, on the other hand, was the worrywart, pointing out the obstacles along the way.

While we were still students at the London School of Economics, Julio had decided he wanted to live in Beijing. He'd found applications open for paid internships in China funded by the European Union. Although he met several of the application criteria, I'd been quick to point out that he had no work experience, while it was clearly mentioned that at least two years of professional experience was necessary. Julio had breezily dismissed my concerns, reasoning that various summer jobs he'd done while at university were enough. I would not have applied for that internship on the basis of Julio's qualifications.

Yet Julio did. And he got it, which allowed him to move to China, for me to follow, and for the rest of our history together to materialize.

It was Julio who had insisted I write a book, even as I hesitated, unsure that I had sufficient authority. He always believed I could write more pieces than I thought I could, and be paid more for them than I was. He was not only more confident about himself than I was about me, but also more confident about me than I was about myself.

Whenever I expressed fears about the professional implications of my pregnancy, he hushed them away. Even as I worried that I was being paid too much for what I was capable of delivering as a pregnant mother of a toddler, he insisted I was being paid tuppence; that my salary made no dent at all in a big newspaper's budget. But I was not totally convinced that he was right.

However unfair it may be, writers don't get paid much and the industry standard sets the context. Freelancers are doubly cursed, paid less than full-time employees and granted few, if any, benefits. Since I was a freelancer, my newspaper was under no obligation to provide me with maternity leave. That they did so was out of the goodness of their hearts rather than contractual necessity. All freelancers are more vulnerable in the workplace, but women even more so.

Kay and Shipman are at pains to explain that the female tendency towards professional under-confidence (which may be both biological and environmental) can be unlearnt through practice and policy. I agree. After all, I had negotiated maternity leave despite the embarrassment and guilt I had felt while doing so. And I'd been determined to ask for a salary rise (gasp!) once I'd finished two years on the job. But it did seem a far more draining experience for me to ask for 'my due' professionally than it ever was for Julio.

Moreover, regardless of the veracity of the confidence gap

hypothesis, the fact was that even I – an avowed feminist, with a career-supporting spouse and an impressive résumé – felt professionally cowed by a pregnancy. Whichever way this was spun, it was not good news for women.

As my pregnancy progressed, so did the déjà vu. The twenty-week ultrasound revealed the somersaulting fetus to be another boy. Once again, Julio and I were at loggerheads, arguing over names. I suggested Armaan and Rehaan. He recoiled in horror, and countered with anachronistic Spanish monikers such as Agapito that were meant to irritate me rather than present realistic options. Julio's father, Julio, reiterated his belief that 'Julio' would be a sound choice. My mother reserved Dhananjay, with a hopeful air. My pregnancy was on repeat.

This felt to be even more the case when I set off for India, on a book tour. Both my books, *Smoke and Mirrors* and *Chinese Whiskers*, were published during the second trimester of my two pregnancies. With my books and babies so tied together, I felt truly fecund.

Julio remained chipper, staying optimistic on the chances of baby number two avoiding colic. Given how reminiscent the second pregnancy was of the first, however, I was increasingly less convinced on the matter.

It was at the start of the third trimester that the two pregnancies began to diverge, but not for the better. I was travelling in China with a seven-month-round belly, attending literature festivals in Beijing and Shanghai to promote *Chinese Whiskers,* when I developed a severe pain in my pelvic joint. I began to find it difficult to walk or even to turn sides in bed.

As soon as I returned to Brussels, I limped my way to my gynaecologist, Dr D, only to have him dismiss my concerns. He listened absent-mindedly to my description of the debilitating pain, before commenting that my symptoms were 'strange'. He then led me to his ultrasound antechamber where he had a 'look' at the fetus and beamingly declared that the baby 'was fine'. With that, I was sent home.

This was very much in keeping with my experience as Dr D's patient from the beginning. When I had told him how sick I was with the constant vomiting in the first trimester, he had conducted an ultrasound and announced that the baby was fine. When I developed a viral infection on my lip that disfigured my face and left me in agony, he did an ultrasound and beamed that the baby was well.

Every time I visited the doctor, I departed feeling either like a hypochondriac, or someone lacking the physical courage required to bear up to a pregnancy. He assumed that all the symptoms I mentioned were 'natural', and as long as the baby was 'fine', no action was required. I was reduced to being a vessel that just had to suck up whatever consequences my body suffered from the pregnancy. The only case for any alleviating intervention in Dr D's eyes was if a problem was detected with the baby, to hell with the vessel.

It dawned on me that Dr D had never been pregnant himself, and his entire conception of what was 'natural' or not was theoretical. My Beijing gynaecologist, Dr Brooks of 'Indian bum' notoriety, had been equally cavalier. I tried discussing my concerns with Julio, only to meet with frustratingly obtuse responses. He agreed that perhaps Dr D was not responsive to my 'emotional' needs, but felt that he was competent medically. Decoded, this meant that while the doctor did not indulge my hysterical, psychosomatic problems, he had a rational and medically sound approach to ensuring a safe pregnancy.

Despite my misgivings, I stuck to Dr D, partly out of inertia, and partly out of the feeling that perhaps Julio and the doctor himself were right. Maybe I was overreacting to the 'normal' effects of pregnancy. Perhaps I just needed to embrace the discomfort and get on with it.

But then my blood sugar levels came back elevated on a standard test. Dr D looked at the results and casually suggested I avoid eating 'too much' sugar for the rest of the pregnancy. He proceeded to do an ultrasound and declare the baby to be 'fine', after which he sent me home with a paternal, and literal, pat on the back. This time, I was not willing to accept his sanguine assurances.

I made an appointment with a highly recommended female obstetrician and gynaecologist who took one look at my test results and ordered a full-scale glucose endurance test. The results were clear. I had gestational diabetes.

Dr D had in fact been hugely negligent in not insisting on a follow-up to my high blood sugar results. His shortcomings were not limited to just a lack of interest in meeting my 'emotional' (read medically extraneous, typically overwrought feminine) needs. He was professionally inept, and my dissatisfaction with his care had strong, rational grounds. In retrospect I am amazed I'd allowed my reasoning to be so easily dismissed by what was essentially male condescension.[2]

The next few weeks were difficult. I had always been needle-phobic, and now I had to prick my own finger to measure blood sugar levels after every meal. It wasn't easy to keep on even keel, but I had help. I met with a dietician who helped me plan meals and an endocrinologist who explained the mechanics of insulin resistance. Pregnancy in the first world was a great privilege.

My new doctor, the mother of three children herself, also immediately prescribed safe, homeopathic remedies for the viral infection that had ravaged my lips. Finally, she addressed my pelvic pain problem, explaining that it was the result of the overproduction of a hormone that softens the ligaments. I was dispatched to a physiotherapist to learn exercises, and receive massage, to manage the pain.

Prenatal and post-natal physiotherapy were considered an essential part of pregnancy-related care in Belgium. The costs for these sessions were covered, in part, by the state. Classes consisted of a series of light exercises to keep the joints limber, in addition to the teaching of techniques to use when pushing during labour. The physiotherapist would also be present during the actual delivery of the baby. Her role at the birth was to support and assist the mother, while the doctor focused on the medical aspects of delivery.

The involvement of the Belgian state with pregnancy care was a pleasant surprise, given that in China all things 'natal' were wholly private (and privately paid for). But in Brussels, I even had the local pharmacy hand me a free 'pregnancy' package, which included labour and breastfeeding information, in addition to samples for various baby products. In physiotherapy, I met other expecting mothers, some of whom shared my pelvic aches, and others who had been similarly afflicted by gestational diabetes. The therapists themselves were gentle and wise. My pregnancy suddenly felt like a community concern.

It was just as well that I had the Belgian state supporting my expanding girth, because it increasingly felt like I did not have a husband. Julio had been swallowed up by work. As was common with parents starting out on family life, the timing was fatal. In his mid-thirties, with just the right amount of maturity and experience, Julio was hitting his professional stride. The European Union was about to establish a brand new diplomatic corps, known by its vowel-heavy acronym, the EEAS (European External

Action Service). Julio was offered a position as assistant of this august institution's chief operating officer (COO).

My spouse was now the chief implementer of a large and ambitious new organization. He was an influential gatekeeper, and gained instant visibility across the sprawling institutions of the European Union. He also had to work all the time.

Despite an 8 a.m. start, it was a rare day that Julio made it home before nine at night, two hours after Ishaan's bedtime. I was abandoned to my pregnancy, and to the care of a toddler who quite probably suffered from oppositional defiant disorder. I was left alone to cope with dinners that left me coated in colourful foods. I wrestled the toothbrush demon out of his bath every evening with solitary effort. I stuffed his kinetic body into pajamas with only the glassy-eyed cats for company. I hauled him up three flights of stairs to his bedroom, and spent an eternity singing songs till he fell asleep. There was no one to give me even an occasional break.

There were times when Ishaan battered me from without, while the baby kicked from within. I felt like a giant, diabetic football. My first pregnancy took on a sepia-tinted glow. I remembered being able to rest when I was tired. There had been solicitous calls from family and friends. Julio had brought me ice cream to eat whenever I'd craved it.

Now, there was no rest, few calls, and nothing sweet; only blood sugar monitoring and a hyperactive toddler. All the attention that was lavished on a first-time pregnancy by well-wishers had evaporated. By the time number two rolled around you were supposed to be a pro. Popping out kids was now assumed to be second nature to you. But in fact a second pregnancy was far harder. There was another, attention-seeking, child to look after. I was, therefore, more tired than before, as well as being older. I suffered from chronic insomnia. And I was, more or less, without a husband.

Disconcertingly, this was a fairly typical experience of motherhood. It was par for the course. If anything, I had it fairly cushy.

During this time I began rereading Nobel Prize–winner Pearl S. Buck's *The Good Earth*, a novel that was set in the hardscrabble Chinese countryside in the early twentieth century. It features O-lan, a slave girl who wins her freedom by marrying a poor peasant. Displaying enormous fortitude and capacity for physical labour, a pregnant O-lan works in the fields until a few hours before she delivers her own baby. Subsequent children are born in similar circumstances. And with each birth, the woman is ever more casual, returning to the fields after barely pausing to rest.

Reading the book made me somewhat ashamed. Many of my complaints amounted to nothing but glorified whingeing. Being a grown-up *is* tough. Having and raising children *is* challenging. In fact a lot of life involves pain and abnegation.

But unlike O-lan, I had grown up at a time, in a culture, and with material circumstances that conspired to airbrush physical discomfort out of the picture. The worst form of corporeal distress that people like me are taught to expect is a long-haul flight in economy class. Happiness, many of us have come to believe, is a state of pleasure entirely divorced from pain.

This ideal of unsullied happiness is our yardstick and guide. 'Do what makes you happy' is the mantra of popular advice. But the nature of 'happiness' goes uninterrogated. There are, after all, so many avatars of happiness. Long-term, hard-won, and profound happiness has little to do with fleeting, reactive and sensory pleasure. And yet, we often conflate them, mindlessly. The result is an elongation of adolescence.

'Growing up', I realized, is not about gaining financial independence, falling in love, or even growing older. It is rather about losing some of the narcissism that is so inherent in our self-regarding culture, celebrating our individual choice. It is about grasping atavistic truths like the importance, not just of choosing what makes one happy, but doing one's duty. It is about losing one's freedom and maintaining, rather than falling in, love. Discovering that 'true' happiness is intertwined with some amount of sacrifice and the giving up of some choices. For me, it turned out to be about having children.

I decided that it would not do to pity myself too much. All mothers are tired, and no pregnant woman has it easy. But the one grouse that I felt was somewhat justified, given the kind of marriage I believed I had entered into, was that of gender equality, or its lack, at home. The lopsided nature of childcare responsibilities, which were heavily stacked against me, was an issue I could be righteously upset about, and so all my varied frustrations coalesced around the matter.

Even if it were 'normal' for me as the pregnant mother of a young child to sacrifice many of my own comforts in the service of procreation, why wasn't the same true of the father? Why did my growing up/motherhood have to embrace physical pain and forbearance, while his growing up/fatherhood featured career success and bodily integrity?

The unhappy result of asking this question was a spike in marital arguments. I felt bewildered at how gendered our home had become. Until Julio's new EEAS job, we had managed a semblance of fairness in childcare. I undertook the lion's share of Ishaan-related work, but Julio was involved in his son's life too. He often picked him up from the day-care centre at the end of the day. He made him breakfast, and read him bedtime stories.

But the new job upturned this precarious equilibrium. Julio rarely saw Ishaan on weekdays now, except for a short spell in the morning during which he was always in a hurry to leave. Breakfast time became stiff with tension. We didn't chat or smile any longer, but barked and sulked instead. I kept thinking that this was not what I had signed up for in marrying, and having children with, Julio.

With the benefit of hindsight, I came to see that it was unreasonable of me to blame Julio. My husband's job required him to work in a manner that was inconsistent with his responsibilities as a father. He therefore had two choices, the same that the majority of people in the workplace face: career satisfaction versus fatherhood/motherhood.

Theoretically, Julio could have simply turned down the EEAS job, which would have allowed him to spend more time with Ishaan, thereby reducing some of the childcare load on me. Weighed up against this were the facts that his work at the EEAS was more stimulating, and afforded him better career prospects.

Julio and I had always wanted our stint in Brussels to be a temporary one. The idea was to move back to Asia if we could swing it. The EEAS job, Julio told me, was our best bet at achieving this goal. It would require a few years of sacrifice and hard work to put him in a position to apply for a post at one of the EU's delegations abroad. He lacked the requisite seniority for many of these positions, but the extra visibility and networking opportunities his new job proffered might make up for this.

Over the years I sat and chatted with mom friends of different nationalities and circumstances in many different parts of the world. We often had divergent experiences and expectations of motherhood. But we were inevitably bound together in having faced this conundrum at home: to have the kind of financial security and future prospects we wanted as a family, at least one spouse needed to work hours that made it impossible for them to take on their full responsibilities as a parent. This was the unyielding reality that many a feminist, man and woman, found their efforts at 'equality' shattering against.

The obvious question was why the spouse who committed

to 'work' rather than to childcare was overwhelmingly the man? When I posed this query to friends, many, often the men, would answer that it was a straightforward matter of money. The men earned more than the women concerned. My male friends sometimes claimed that they would have happily stayed at home to look after the kids had their wives simply pulled in higher salaries.

But why did their wives earn less? The couples I'm talking about were usually educated to the same level. Often they worked in the same profession.

By way of explanation, some husbands said that they were older, and hence senior to their wives at the point when it became necessary for one of them to focus on raising children. Even if this were the case it seemed profoundly unfair to freeze people's opportunities for much of their productive lives on the basis of a few years' age difference. But, the crux of the matter, of course, was unrelated to one's year of birth.

Women, everywhere, are paid less than men, the result of workplace discrimination that results from a mix of cultural and policy variables. This is true of developed and developing countries. Geographical, religious and economic variations across the countries of the world have an impact on just how egregious this pay gap is. And yet, nowhere has this gap been successfully closed, even as other gulfs, such as those pertaining to education have almost disappeared.[3] Many employers continue to look upon salaries for women as extra pocket money, rather than the mainstay of income for their families. I have friends who had been asked pointed questions about their husband's jobs while interviewing for vacancies themselves. The point of this line of questioning was rarely made explicit, but the reasons were loud and clear nonetheless.

There were many other explanations too, all of them valid for illustrating some aspect of the gender wage gap. In her bestselling book, *Lean In*, Facebook COO Sheryl Sandberg writes that she had repeatedly seen women sabotaging their own career prospects by settling for lower-paid and less ambitious jobs, rather than applying for more challenging positions, even before they became mothers. They made these choices in preparation for having children at some point down the line.[4] In effect, they pre-emptively amputated their careers.

Women also tend to choose lower-paying, but more flexible, stable or emotionally rewarding careers in 'pink' professions like teaching and development work, rather than the 'hard', highly remunerative worlds of finance, technology or engineering.

I had studied philosophy at university despite scoring some of the highest school-leaving examination results in the country. The 'cut off' percentage for a degree in philosophy at Delhi University was amongst the lowest for the subjects on offer for an honours BA degree. The reason, I assume, is the lack of earning potential associated with someone conversant in philosophy, compared to someone with a background in economics or physics. And yet, I'd plumped for philosophy without hesitation.

This was largely because I hadn't been remotely concerned with factoring in my future earnings as a variable in the decision. Instead, I'd made my choice wholly on the basis of what I thought would be interesting. Did this decision have something to do with my gender? Would I have chosen differently had I been brought up as a boy? It is certainly possible. Gender was not a conscious factor in my choice of study. But I'm not sure it would have been as easy for a man to be as blithely disregarding of the financial implications of that choice.

Other friends hypothesized that the reason was biological. That children, especially young ones, needed and desired their mothers more than their fathers. Breastfeeding was a staple of this explanation. Its corollary was that mothers enjoyed spending time with their children more than dads and were better suited temperamentally, being 'natural' nurturers, than men.

My reaction to that particular argument was that I had hated breastfeeding and not done any beyond three months with Ishaan. I was also far more 'naturally' inclined to spend time with adults. Being feted as a writer and analyst of world affairs was more enjoyable for me than wiping the drool off a red-faced mite. Also, although children did turn to their mothers more often than their fathers, this might have something to do with the fact that their mothers were usually more available.

I did not buy the claims of those male friends who avowed they would love to stay at home looking after their children, if only their wives earned more money. Caring for a child round the clock is very dull, even if it offers transcendental moments of joy. I suspect the truth is that most modern dads would very much like to keep their professional jobs, but would also like to spend some more time with their children. In short, they would like some work–life balance. 'Having it all' is not only a woman's issue.

And so, for all my feminist instincts, I found myself complicit in what had evolved into a more 'traditional' domestic arrangement than I'd ever imagined I'd be part of. I agreed that Julio's new job was the best option for the family as a whole, even if it meant that I would be saddled with more domestic responsibilities, and left with less time in which to pursue my professional work. But then, I reasoned, if Julio's job were to eventually allow us to move to Asia, it would help my future career goals, since this was the part of the world I most wanted to write about. It seemed to be a reasonable compromise to make. And it was. But as with all trade-offs there were also unforeseen consequences.

Once a pattern of parental interaction is established, it becomes very difficult to alter later on. Julio's absence from so much of Ishaan's early childhood affected their relationship further down the line as well. Ishaan came to automatically look to me rather than his father. When he wanted to share his fears and desires, it was I who was physically present. When he needed help finding his socks, it was also I who was physically present. Small wonder, therefore, that the synchronicity between Ishaan and me eluded Julio, even after changed professional circumstances allowed him to spend more time at home.

By April 2011, I took leave from the newspaper, two months earlier than I'd planned. I felt incapable of juggling all the balls I had been doing. The diabetes diagnosis was the straw that broke my pregnant back. Having to draw blood to test sugar levels all day, combined with constant meal planning, was draining. I was weepy much of the time. At other times I found myself contemplating mortality. Experiences like pregnancy, and giving birth, which are so viscerally physical, have that effect. They force us to confront our essential frailty. Our blink-and-you're-gone reality.

Fortunately, other realities, like potty training, kept me from getting too morbid. Ishaan was approaching his third birthday and still showed no signs of dispensing with diapers. I read him endless potty-related books. I tried bribing him with M&Ms. I threatened him with dire consequences, the precise nature of which I forget. I promised him golden star stickers for cooperation. I bought a portable toilet with the Disney character Lightning McQueen (whom I abhorred as much as Ishaan loved) painted all over it. But Ishaan treated blandishments and coercion with equal scorn.

My German friend's daughter, Kathy, might have had no knowledge of Mozart, but she had been using the toilet since she was twenty months old. Girls 'trained' faster than boys, everyone agreed, but just how much longer would Ishaan take?

The crèche was not much help either. When I brought up my concerns about Ishaan's 'delay' with his teachers, they suggested I meet with the day-care centre's psychopedagogue. This sounded rather insulting. I may have been stressed, but was not yet certifiable. I calmed down once Julio explained that a psycho-pedagogue was not someone who treated psychotic mothers, but merely the French term for an expert in child development and behaviour.

At our meeting, the psycho-pedagogue handed me a stapled copy of voluminous photocopied material on potty training, all of which boiled down to advising parents not to worry. 'When the child is ready, the child will go to the toilet,' she insisted in a tone that brooked no dissent. And that was that.

I was miffed. In India, babies were often out of diapers before they were walking.

In China, babies and toddlers were commonly dressed in trousers called *kaidangku*, or open-crotch pants, where a split over the buttocks area allowed the child to 'use the loo' without the need for lowering them. Parents sometimes allowed their children to make use of their kaidangku on street pavements and occasionally even on supermarket floors. Diapers were not part of the equation.

In Beijing, we had not gone in for the bare-bottom look or associated practices of a kaidangku. But Auntie Mei had other tricks up her sleeve. She would surreptitiously divest the infant Ishaan of his diapers and hold him over the bucket that was usually used for handwashing clothes, while fiercely hissing 'sssssssss'. The first time I stumbled upon her thus, she'd looked at me defiantly. 'What? Soon he won't need diapers. You'll save a lot of money.'

It required considerable adult intervention and cleaning up for early toilet training to succeed. In societies where most people could not afford disposable diapers there was obviously a greater incentive to make this effort. In Europe, the combination of richer families and less help for mothers meant that toilet training was easier postponed. Consequently, while all the two-year-olds in Ishaan's crèche were able to independently use a fork and spoon with reasonable felicity, most of them were still in diapers. In India and China, the toddler norm was the opposite.

In Ishaan's case, the crèche psycho-pedagogue was eventually proved right. One month shy of his third birthday Ishaan used the toilet, and that was that.

My son's new potty-using skills were not the only phenomenon that gave me some respite from pregnancy woes. He had also begun to talk, and talk. And while his constant chatter could be infuriating, it could also crack me up. Ishaan was sassy and idiosyncratic. He often managed to pierce through my gloomiest moods with a single sentence or two.

He could be poetic, as in when he insisted on carrying a pair of dark glasses to crèche one morning. I began to respond with my Harvey Karp techniques but the toddlerese was cut short when he explained the necessity of the request. 'You see, otherwise the summer will get in my eyes,' he said solemnly.

He could be a nationalist. Although Ishaan always claimed to be Chinese when asked where he was from, he was inexplicably whimsical one evening. 'You know what I think, Mama?' he asked. 'Hmm?' I said absent-mindedly. 'I think that the moon is Indian,' he replied with a firm nod of his head.

He was always brutally honest. Once when I had a friend from down the road visit, he walked in on us having a cup of tea and said to our guest, 'Can you go home now?' In shocked tones I hushed him and told him not to be so rude. Ishaan turned to my friend again, and corrected himself: 'Can you go home now, please?'

He could be downright hilarious. Exhausted by his constant arguing, negotiating, and inability to just accept my utterances as commands (motherhood has engendered a great sympathy for dictatorship in me), I clutched my hair in despair one evening and groaned, 'Oh Ishaaaaan, I am so sick of being a mother.'

'Really?' he asked solicitously. 'Would you rather be a pirate instead?'

It had become very uncomfortable for me to laugh too hard at Ishaan's aphorisms though, as I approached my thirty-sixth week of pregnancy. Because of the strict diet I was on, I hadn't put on too much weight, and yet I felt stretched to breaking point. The ripples of the baby's movements under my taut belly could now be seen, not only felt. I couldn't help feeling there was something a tad grotesque about them. They were suggestive of monsters lurking in the deeps. But it was only little Nicolas.

Julio and I had finally managed to agree on a name for number two. I'd scoured my husband's family tree for male names that were not Julio, and found Nicolas. Shortened to Nico, it was sweet, and it mollified my father-in-law.

But three weeks before my due date, my gynaecologist was grim-faced as she patted down my tummy. Nico was in a breech position and it was likely I would need a C-section. Unless, she continued, I agreed to her trying out an external manipulation in which she would try to physically turn the baby the right way down. The procedure would need to be done in hospital, and only had a 50 per cent chance of success.

I agreed without hesitation. The last thing I wanted was for my body to be cut open and to have to deal with recovery from surgery, in addition to the mayhem that a newborn inevitably unleashed.

The next day, I momentarily regretted my decision, as I lay supine while hooked up to an intravenous drip and fetal-monitoring device. It turned out that the 'external' manipulation was somewhat euphemistic. The reality involved both external and *internal* manoeuvring on the part of the doctor. It was not exactly painful, but extremely creepy. Luckily, it lasted only ten minutes and in the moment before my gynaecologist was about to give up, Nico finally obliged and turned head down.

I'm convinced that had Ishaan been in similar circumstances he'd have refused. Nico was a more accommodating child. His yielding to the doctor's manipulations was the first indication I had of this.

I was back home an hour later. The doctor was relieved that in all likelihood a C-section would now be avoided. However, labour might start earlier than expected, she warned. Her 'external' interventions had already stirred Nico into action.

And so, a few days later, I awoke one morning to another 'bloody show'. This time my birth plan was different from what it had been in Beijing, given that the prevalent attitude to childbirth in Belgium was radically different from the American Earth Mother who had been my primary advisor in China.

I had been on a hospital tour a month earlier and been told in no uncertain terms by the staff to check in as soon as my contractions began. Do not delay, I was advised in direct contra-indication to the 'hold on till the last minute possible' strategy I'd been urged to employ with Ishaan. That I would be getting an epidural was also assumed rather than discussed. The hospital I was going to give birth in was one of Brussels' best. More than 90 per cent of women who delivered babies there received epidurals.

On the day of the 'bloody show', I began to have light contractions by mid-morning. I called Julio at work and he took the rest of the day off. We went to a neighbourhood Italian restaurant for a light lunch before heading to the hospital. Ishaan was still at crèche. We had arranged for our nanny to stay the night with him, but I was stressed about the arrangement.

I didn't know what Ishaan would make of our sudden absence. He'd never spent a night away from both Julio and me before. I'd been trying to talk to him about the imminent arrival of his baby brother for months, but he'd never seemed particularly interested. At best he'd been indulgently dismissive, in a 'There's a baby in your tummy? Right! What have you been smoking?' kind of way.

At the hospital I had barely settled into my delivery room when the midwife asked if I'd like an epidural. I hesitated. I did not particularly want to experience the agony of childbirth. I also did not want to delay pain medication to the ridiculous extent I had done with Ishaan. And yet, there was such horror in the idea of a needle puncturing my spine.

Julio explained my dilemma to the midwife: 'She wants one, but she's scared of the needle.' 'Well then,' the matronly lady replied briskly, 'we'd best get on with it.' Five minutes later, an anaesthetist sauntered in with evil-looking syringe and tube equipment. I was helped up into sitting position. My heart galloped as I squeezed my eyes shut and tried to calm myself. Through the waves of panic I overheard the anaesthetist casually chatting with Julio in French. 'Is she Sri Lankan,' he asked my spouse, as though I were not in the room.

When Julio told him I was Indian, he grunted. 'Must be from the south?' he continued, rummaging about his materials interminably. 'She's quite dark.' How I wanted to smack the man. Hard. But he was approaching my spine with a huge needle and I decided it wasn't the best time to become confrontational.

Thankfully, within a minute, it was all over. The epidural was administered, the idiotic anaesthetist had left, and the pain of the contractions had vanished. I sank back in bed feeling euphoric at the sudden absence of pain. Julio put on a Joaquin Sabina CD. The midwife left us alone. I snoozed for a while.

Then suddenly, it was time for business. The midwife was back and after a brisk examination she announced that the pushing stage was nigh. She made a few calls and my gynaecologist and physiotherapist appeared, even though it was close to midnight. The room was filled with music and feminine support. The physio reminded me gently of the pushing exercises we had practised. The doctor congratulated me on my sterling effort with every thrust. I smiled through the whole process, aware of the contractions, but in no pain.

After about fifteen minutes, Nico slipped out and in a jiffy he was in my arms, crinkled and shivering. Julio stood next to us looking pale, but beaming. 'What a peaceful delivery,' the gynaecologist remarked. And it had been.

Other than the Dr D fiasco, I really appreciated the Belgian way, when it came to all things pregnancy- and baby-related: the state-funded physiotherapists, the laissez-faire attitudc towards potty training, the lack of angst regarding taking epidurals – all combined for a more comfortable and less guilty experience of matters natal than those advocated by my Beijing-based American midwife's 'natural' childbirth philosophy.

Perhaps American journalist Pamela Druckerman, was on to something in her 'the French do it better' book on parenting, *Bringing Up Bebe.*[5] The book played on the cultural anxieties of many American parents by claiming that the French brought up better-mannered and more socially adjusted children than their trans-Atlantic counterparts. While much of the reasoning in support of these claims was based on too wide generalizations, the state support for French mothers was a solid difference. Unlike in the US (and many other countries), in France, there was national paid maternity leave, subsidies for nannies and quality day care, as well as free preschool. These were all policies that Belgium shared.

I spent the next five days in relative isolation at the hospital. In many countries mothers were sent home almost as soon as they had given birth. But in Belgium, a a five- or six-day hospital stay was strongly advised. During this time nurses and lactation specialists assisted with breastfeeding and other infant care. The physio came by to start the mom on post-natal exercises aimed at recovering pelvic and abdominal muscle tone. It was advised to keep visitors to the minimum to allow the mother and baby to bond in a quiet environment.

The post-natal moment that stayed with me the longest was Ishaan's reaction to meeting his new brother. He came running into the room, joyfully calling out 'Mama'! It had been more than twenty-four hours since he had last set eyes on me. A long time by his book. But when he saw me reclining on the hospital bed with a baby suckling at my breast, he looked stricken and let out a short, sharp yelp. It was a cry of visceral sorrow, as though he realized at some primal level that life, as he had known it, was over. There was competition now and it was here to stay.

In later months and years when I queried him on this reaction, Ishaan was dismissive. 'It was just that I wasn't expecting Nico to be there,' he'd explain.

6

VALUE

2011–12, BRUSSELS

By the time Nico was four months old, I was champing at the bit to be back at work. In the history of random coincidences an honourable mention belongs to that of my pregnancies and the impending economic implosion of the Western world. The collapse of investment banking behemoth Lehman Brothers in the same month as Ishaan's birth in September 2008 had left global markets in turmoil. Three years later, as Nico emerged into the world, plangent obituaries were being written about the eurozone.

A sovereign debt crisis in Greece that had come to light in 2010 had proved infectious, and fiscal contagion was fast spreading across the seventeen countries that used the euro currency. There were fears of a double-dip recession, and talk of Europe's 'Lehman moment'.

All of which meant that being the Europe correspondent of a business newspaper, even an Indian one, was suddenly a substantial job. I had imagined that the move from Beijing to Brussels would be mirrored by a shift from the front pages to journalistic obscurity. Instead, I had once again found myself in the eye of a news maelstrom. I no longer had a ringside view of the Rise of China, but I certainly had managed front-row seats to the Decline of Europe, an unexpected bonanza for any enthusiastic journalist. And yet, I'd spent months-worth of the 'story' doing scant but breastfeeding.

I had in fact been breastfeeding as relentlessly as the fiscal and banking crisis was sweeping across the eurozone. On the day I discovered that I was pregnant with a second child, I decided that this time round I would breastfeed until the cows came home, at the risk of transforming into a cow myself. I refused to give in to formula and face a repeat of the all-consuming guilt of failure I had nearly drowned in with Ishaan.

I primed myself to be calm and expect little from the first few weeks of Nico's life, save pain, boredom and endless suckling. But there came a moment when desperate to give my sore mammaries a rest from the infant's rock-hard gums, I brought out the old breast pump and gave it a mechanical shot. As had been my experience with Ishaan, I found it impossible to coax out milk in any meaningful quantity, and was immediately filled with a familiar depression.

Nico was a tiny baby, of well below average weight according to Western standards. I was aware that Indian babies tended to be smaller than their European cousins, but my lack of success with pumping led to a host of familiar worries. Was I starving my little one? Was the La Leche League's insistence that there was no such thing as a low milk supply really true?

Nico was gaining just enough weight every week for the paediatrician to advise that I persist with breastfeeding, and so I buried the pump in the dark recesses of a closet, determined never to subject myself to its humiliating ministrations again. I would just have to trust my body, as the La Leche League always advised.

It wasn't easy. Predictably, Nico was 'colicky'. He cried, occasionally for hours. He slept in short bursts and never calmly watched the world go by while reclining in his stroller. Instead, he bucked and twisted. He needed swaddling, shushing and rocking, Harvey Karp–style, to fall asleep. Our hairdryer was pressed back into service to create the ambient white noise that seemed to help my offspring slumber deeper and longer.

And yet, the overall tenor of those first few months was less apocalyptic with Nico than it had been with Ishaan. I think this is what people meant when they said it is 'easier' with a second child. For us it was easier, simply because now I knew that every phase a child goes through passes. At some point, even if it was a long way down the road, Nico would sleep through the night. One day he would make a drawing. And some day he would crack a joke.

But it wasn't easier in any other manner. Two children seemed to me to be four times the work. For the next few years childcare was a relay race without a finishing line. When one child napped, the other wanted to play. When one started to recover from a cold, the other came down with a tummy upset. When one progressed the other regressed.

Until Nico was born it had been possible to steal moments of leisure. Julio might take Ishaan to the park on a Sunday afternoon and I could spend an hour reading a novel. Or I might finish a report earlier than expected while Ishaan was still at crèche, allowing me time to tarry by the window overlooking the cherry tree in the backyard. With Nico on the scene, every moment of time got divided into an unbending work–child binary. Down time was the great casualty and exhaustion became an ever more frequent companion.

It is small wonder that more women with two kids than those with one leave the workforce. 'It's called the second child hump,' a journalist friend, who was pregnant with her number two, explained to me. Studies have found that it is managing work, a toddler, and a baby that defeats most women, even those who had managed to juggle their career and single child until then.[1]

Suddenly, I began to notice articles that talked about the nail in the coffin of careers, including writerly ones, that second children were. Alice Walker famously said a writer should have only one child 'because with one you can move. With two you are a sitting duck.'[2] And it transpired that a disproportionately large number of successful women writers had stopped at a single child: Susan Sontag, Joan Didion, Mary McCarthy, Elizabeth Hardwick, Margaret Atwood, Ellen Willis and more, according to an article in *The Atlantic* magazine titled, 'The Secret to Being Both a Successful Writer and a Mother: Have Just One Kid.'[3]

Oh Lord, what had I done? Alice Walker had correctly identified me as a 'sitting duck', and quacking was about all I felt good for.

Our decision to have a second had been quite careless. And I held the European Commission at least partly responsible. Even as families in China were forced by state policy to have a single child and many of my friends in India had voluntarily decided on one, our friends in the European Commission thought nothing of three. One Spanish couple had four because they preferred 'even numbers'. Another notoriously fecund pair had eight! The father had to get a special licence to drive the mini bus needed to cart the family about Brussels.

India and China were overpopulated. Governments in these countries either mandated or nudged citizens to have fewer children. Amongst my friends in India it was considered uncouth to have large families. But given their declining demographics, several countries in the European Union did little to discourage people from reproducing.[4] In Belgium, for example, families with three or more children receive large tax benefits.

For employees of the European Commission, every extra child results in an extra financial allowance. Maternity leave is generous. (The European civil servant with eight children had been on maternity leave eight times, although I heard that the administrative department had stopped sending her congratulatory notes on the birth of her children after the fifth baby.) On foreign postings, Commission employees are entitled to homes with extra rooms, extra cupboards and even extra lamps, depending on the number of children they have.

My social circle in Brussels was full of women with multiple children. I only had two. I told myself to stop fussing and made a conscious decision to embrace the new baby experience that so many moms seemed to enjoy. When Ishaan was an infant I had dissipated a lot of energy in trying to get away from him. In carving out little bubbles of time and space that were baby-free. With Nico, I strived for the opposite. I was resolute in cherishing my maternity leave as a time when my only 'job' was to bond with the baby.

I marched down the road to attachment parenting with resolve. I carried Nico around all day in a cloth sling, which allowed him easy access for frequent feedings. At night I slept with him, or more accurately lay awake while he slept next to me. During the day I walked him up and down parks. I even took him on bus rides so that I could feel more empowered by exploring further afield.

I'd never been good with the paraphernalia of babydom: strollers, car seats, rain covers. Watching European women haul infant-bearing car seats with one hand, while pushing toddler-occupied double strollers with the other, left me feeling abject and useless. Just as I found something tyrannical about cooking stoves and washing machines, so I experienced most baby equipment as harrowing. I did try to practise, but inevitably I was unable to collapse our stroller for storage at crucial junctures, or to correctly retract the car seat hood. I never managed, even once, to lift out our expensive 'convertible' car seat and attach it on to the stroller frame with anything resembling the fluidity of the average European mom.

I found getting on and off public transport with the baby particularly testing. Partly I lacked the physical strength, and partly the technique. I came from a class of person in India who did not use buses or metros. The children I'd seen while growing up had been carried around by nannies, and transported longer distances in private cars. The nanny's lap was their car seat. The nanny's arms constituted their stroller. There was no such thing as a rain cover because if it rained the baby was not taken out.

In fact in neither India nor China were women expected to be marching around outdoors with their newborns. It is traditional in both cultures for mothers to be confined in the first few weeks post-partum. In China this is called *zuo yue zi*, literally, sitting the month. The idea is that women who have just given birth are susceptible to infection and need to rest to recover their strength.

At its extreme, women who are zuo yue zi are supposed to refrain from bathing or even brushing teeth. Such zealousness is a rarity these days, but much less is expected of new mothers in Asian cultures compared to Europe. While Indian and Chinese moms are usually being fussed over by relatives as they recline in bed, European ones are often out jogging while pushing sturdy strollers. Their competence is awesome.

I had tried to ignore my own frailties when Ishaan was a baby, but Nico's birth was an opportunity, I believed, to 'fix' my shortcomings. I needed to stop being cowed by strollers. I had interviewed princes and heads of government. I could take a baby out on a bus. And I did. But it was never stress-free. I couldn't locate the pram brakes when I needed to. I nearly spilled Nico out on to the concrete pavement while hurriedly getting off at the bus stop.

Once, I took Nico for a bus ride to an English-language bookstore across town. It was meant to be a treat for me. But in the event I spent the entire miserable twenty minutes at the shop trying to calm the baby's loud crying by surreptitiously breastfeeding as I swayed him about in a sling. It was torture being surrounded by row after row of books that I could have read, if not written, had I still any brains that were not mushy with breast milk left. But, for now I had to make do with glimpses of book covers before hurrying home via another tension-filled bus ride in time for Nico's nap.

When the baby was only a few weeks old I had a visitor from India over for dinner. She was a close friend from my high school days who had subsequently, and coincidentally, gone to university in England with Julio. The friend was on summer vacation in Europe along with her husband and two young children, each a year older than mine.

She arrived shiny and fresh with her family at 8 p.m. My brood had just been put to bed and I felt wrung out like a wet dishcloth. When I asked her how she was coping on a 'holiday' with two little ones, her answer left me goggle-eyed. 'We like to take the kids on summer trips with us,' she said, smiling airily. 'It's the only time in the year we really look after them, so it's good for all of us, you know?'

I didn't know, so I asked her to elaborate.

'You know, in Delhi the nanny gives them their bath every day and all their meals, and we hardly interact with them. Except to play. So, it's nice to spend a few weeks when it's just us looking after them,' my friend explained. She frowned with concern as she continued. 'But, what about you, Pallavi? How on earth do *you* cope over here?'

She pointed towards the living-room floor as she said the word, 'here', her tone somewhere between horror and curiosity. 'Here' was the middle-class, developed world. 'Here' was where mothers (or fathers) gave their own kids baths every single evening of every single week of every single month of every single year.

Talking with my friend made me feel 'Europeanly' superior for a brief while. Hmph! I whispered to myself in the time-honoured tradition of self-righteous mothers: why bother having children at all when you can't be bothered looking after them?

But the truth was that despite my determination to embrace my inner nurturer, what I really wanted was to hand Nico to a nanny and get back to work. At this point, 'work' was a misnomer. 'Work' could have easily swapped labels with 'fun'. The idea of spending a few baby-less hours thinking about Angela Merkel's relationship with the European Central Bank was scintillating.

None of this is to ignore the profound, almost sacred, pleasure that the children could give me. There were times when smelling Nico's breath as his chest rose and fell in his sleep gave me pins and needles of pleasure. I felt like a sufi mystic drunk on God's love. Every day the sublime lurked in the mundane: cracking up over Ishaan's latest joke, cheek-to-cheek naps with Nico, the wild happiness of chasing a soap bubble. But for all these delights there were also hours and hours of whining and shrieking and unreasonable obstinacy.

There was, in addition, another reason for my keenness to return to the desk. This one was financial. Since I'd taken the last two months of my pregnancy off from work, my three months of paid maternity leave only covered a single month post-partum. Therefore, I'd been without a salary for three months already. For the first time since I had met Julio at university, he was the sole earner in our partnership.

Given that we had been married for six years and shared two children, it might have struck some people as odd that we did not share a bank account. But the need for one had never occurred. I paid my own way when it came to personal expenses from clothing to lunch with friends, and Julio paid his. I paid for the house help, he took care of the mortgage. For joint expenses like groceries, we tended to take turns. The financial architecture of our relationship had evolved organically, without much discussion about the main part.

But suddenly, I was without a source of income. This was a state of affairs that left me ontologically wobbly. I had been brought up in an India where the state did not provide any social security net. My family came from a salaried, professional background with scant assets to their name. We literally lived on what we earned. My parents had divorced when I was still a little girl, and my mother had always been anxious about her job, the income from which was what kept her, and me, afloat. A regular income was therefore very much bound up with feelings of emotional stability for me.

I continued to behave financially as though nothing had changed for the three months that I had no salary, including paying for the nanny from my savings. It was only for a short while, I reasoned, and somehow the idea of Julio having to be the provider was invalid, given who I was, or rather, who we were.

My back-to-work plan ran into an unexpected obstacle, however, in Nico's absolutist refusal to countenance a bottle. Since I had eschewed formula entirely, in addition to banishing the breast pump, the only nipple Nico had encountered until this point was mine. And he seemed nonplussed at the silicone one that was now being proffered to him. I retrieved the pump and tried tempting him with breast milk (eked out over several pumping sessions) in the bottle, only to have Nico jerk his head aside in the type of disgust one might imagine a bloody steak to elicit in a vegetarian. Formula met with a similar fate.

This was a nightmare. Here I was, primed for my return to the trenches of the world of news, and my baby refused to take to a bottle. I felt felled by friendly fire. What on earth was I going to do? I cast around desperately for advice on Facebook and was flooded with sympathetic responses from friends who had faced a similar crisis.

A cousin tried to 'comfort' me with the information that by the time her child was *fifteen months* old he'd eventually taken a bottle. An aunt claimed it would help if I faced the baby away from me when offering formula. Others recommended I have Julio give the bottle. I was advised to stay out of the room while a feed was attempted. I was counselled to stay out of the house altogether.

A horrible, horrible, week followed during which I spent a few hours a day cowering at the media centre at the European Union headquarters, unable to focus on the press conferences swirling around me, convinced that I was the cruellest mother alive. I was starving my child by denying him the breast, so that I could work. This was the very definition of the 'bad mother'. I was the vilest of beings, at the top of the taxonomy of evil: a mother who put her own needs ahead of her baby's.

I went around with a gnawing pit in my stomach. But just as I was about to give up and accept life as Nico's permanent feeding machine, he relented. One afternoon, as I listlessly tapped away at the keyboard of my laptop in the EU press room, I received an excited phone call from our nanny. Nico had finally guzzled a bottle down and promptly fallen asleep.

And just like that, all was well again. For a few weeks.

The euro crisis had resulted in a feast of Brussels-based summitry with Europe's great and good – Merkel, Sarkozy, Cameron and friends – revolving in and out of the Belgian capital. All eyes were on Germany, the Union's austere new boss, and whether or not it would allow bailouts of the eurozone's weaker economies.

I had lots of reporting to busy myself with, none of which involved travel. Everything was proceeding rather nicely. A new editor took over charge of the paper in Delhi and suggested that I begin writing a monthly column in addition to my reporting beat. I accepted with alacrity. It appeared that I had worried without cause, and I berated myself for lacking confidence.

But barely had my first column been written when I got the phone call I had imagined, and feared, ever since having become a mother: The newspaper was in financial difficulties.[5] I was getting the axe. It was nothing personal. I was brilliant, etc. But, circumstances, etc. Two months' notice. Good luck.

I remember feeling very cold when the phone call ended. I was an award-winning journalist and I'd just been sacked. Sacked. The word thwacked down on my consciousness like an annihilating boulder. I felt unmoored, discombobulated. A job (and a salary) was intrinsic to my identity, so the news felt of existential import.

This reaction was a tad over the top. I had savings, a husband with a stable and well-compensated job, two healthy children, two rotund cats, and even a new book project (having recently signed a publishing contract to write about Europe's various crises). Losing the newspaper position was not a matter of life and death. And yet, without it, I did not feel 'me'.

Thankfully, I was eventually able to discover a more durable, if less well paid, sense of self, but at the time I was wracked by the questions: Was it my pregnancies/babies that had somehow 'caused' the lay off? Had I been rendered more dispensable by motherhood? Had my children been seen as competition to my commitment to work? Did the fact that I had just taken six months of maternity leave, in the middle of the euro crisis, have anything to do with the axe falling on my neck?

It is difficult to know with certainty, but I tend to think not. Purse strings were being pulled tighter across the newspaper industry. My newspaper hadn't had a Europe correspondent before me, and nor did it hire a replacement after I was cast off. Taking me on had been a luxury for them, and closing me down was a relatively painless way to make some savings. In fact, it's possible that my pregnancy had actually gained me a few extra months of employment. After all, firing a pregnant woman would be scandalous.

But, regardless of the motivations behind the decision, the result was that I had gone from a remunerative peak in the period just before my first child, to a salary cut once Ishaan was born, to no salary or job, now that I was the mother of two. It was a spectacular descent. I wallowed in misery for a few weeks before deciding to look on the proverbial bright side. After all, I could now stop ignoring the impossibility of writing my new book.

The genesis of the said book had its origins in a relatively idle week during my maternity leave. I had devised a proposal to unpack some of the overlapping layers of the challenges that collectively constituted the 'crisis' facing contemporary Europe. I was going to approach this broad and somewhat dense topic from a Chinese–Indian perspective. My email to a publisher met with an unexpectedly prompt and enthusiastic response. And while I'd been momentarily excited, I'd spent most of my time since then avoiding confronting the two children and full-time job-shaped fact, that given my circumstances, it was a nigh on impossible task.

I was a relative novice to the region and needed to read extensively across a spectrum of issues, in addition to tailor-made reportage and travel. This would have been a daunting task for even the most unencumbered of writers. For the mother of an infant and a toddler who was also trying to hold down a reporting job, it was as likely a possibility as getting a full night's sleep.

I had written *Smoke and Mirrors* during the evenings and on weekends, and finished the actual writing in six months flat. By the time I had started on *Chinese Whiskers*, Ishaan's arrival had ensured that I could no longer write on weekends. The novel, which I'd started working on while still on maternity leave, was therefore finished on slow news days, of which there were several in Brussels prior to the euro crisis. *Chinese Whiskers* was a short book. Nonetheless, it had taken me fifteen months to finish.

The Europe book, eventually titled *Punjabi Parmesan:*

Dispatches from a Europe in Crisis, was to take me twenty-two months to write. For eighteen of these months, I did not hold down an additional job outside of the home. If I hadn't lost my job when I did, it is probable that *Punjabi Parmesan* would not have made it to the printing press. Sometimes, you need to be rescued from 'having it all'.

It was Julio who encouraged me to feel liberated by the lay-off and to go travelling on book research instead of lamenting my joblessness. Once again he proved that although he might not always have lived up to my parenting ideals, my husband was the best thing that had ever happened to my career.

Over the next few months I made several short excursions around Europe. I travelled with a group of ten-year-olds from China on a skiing vacation in Austria to help me understand how future generations of Chinese might view Europe. I went to Germany to research the country's profitable small and medium enterprises or Mittelstand, as I grappled with the question of how the German economy had managed to buck the broader European trend of decline. I visited Bordeaux, in France, to meet with the new Chinese wine barons in the region. And I flew to Italy to interview the Punjabi farmhands who provided the labour for much of the Italian dairy and agricultural sectors (hence the title of the new book – *Punjabi Parmesan*).

Fortunately, foreign rights to *Chinese Whiskers* had recently been sold to publishers in several countries, and so I had enough cash to fund these travels. I also wrote short newspaper and magazine features based on this reportage and hawked them for a couple of hundred dollars here and there.

My greatest challenge, during this time, was in mentally decoupling the idea of 'value' from money. Looking after my children and writing books that allowed me to tackle interesting issues in depth were both valuable pursuits to me. Yet their monetary value was nil and negligible, respectively. Reporting, while the least personally valuable of the three pillars in my work–life equation, was, nonetheless, the best remunerated financially.

The problem of 'value' lay at the heart of many gender-related issues. The idea that housework needs to be given a monetary value to expose the dependence of the formal economy on the unpaid and unacknowledged labour of caregivers, overwhelmingly women, has a long history. The best-known articulation of this concept was in the 1970s Wages for Housework Campaign by Marxist feminists like Selma James, Brigitte Galtier, Mariarosa Dalla Costa and Silvia Federici.[6]

But campaigns like these only posed philosophical conundrums about how 'value' is judged. Is value particular, or universal? Is value intrinsic to a 'thing' itself, or is it something that is awarded by an extrinsic assessor?

There are complexities in the duality of the word, because value can have both a moral and monetary iteration. A diamond is valuable because it costs a lot of money, while kindness is valuable because it is moral. In monetary terms investment bankers are more valued than nuns; but many people would agree that Mother Teresa's contribution to society has been more valuable than Dick Fuld's.

'Value' is a capacious term and encompasses categories that are difficult to compare, like the material and the emotional. The moral variant of 'value' is more obviously subjective, open to debate and cultural relativism. The monetary one seems more objective. The price of a diamond is fixed and quantifiable, but the value of parenting is not.

It is telling, in retrospect, how over the next year I described myself to others as being on a break from 'work'. 'I'm on a sabbatical,' I would say, stressing the temporariness of my jobless status. And yet, I was writing a book, and looking after two children under the age of four. I was working harder than I had ever before, but I did not consider my labours to qualify as 'work', because I was not drawing a regular salary.

I realized how much I had linked the idea of value with money. Money's role in evaluating self-worth is crucial and yet somewhat opaque. I read the nineteenth-century German thinker George Simmel on the subject.

Simmel's classic text, *The Philosophy of Money*, describes how money's role in human society arose from the need to find a supposedly 'objective' way of allowing us to compare otherwise incommensurate objects.[7] For example, a haircut, a heart transplant, an African safari and a book can all be compared on the basis of their monetary value, despite belonging to different categories of objects.

Yet, although money itself might be a neutral measure, the value system that underlies our money-based economy is far from purely rational or objective. The huge gulf in the earnings of a sanitation worker and a movie actor, for instance, is hardly indicative of their 'objective' worth. Even the value of physical objects like commodities and 'financial' objects like stocks and collateralized debt obligations can fluctuate wildly because of factors that have little to do with their intrinsic worth. The monetary value assigned to them is not the result of a wholly neutral or rational process, but influenced by the subjective actions of those in positions of power. Greed and self-interest have a role in this.

Yet, money remains the most reliable and accepted definer of value we have. As a result, non-financially remunerated work, like that undertaken by stay-at-home parents, is devalued, regardless of how critical for society it is.

The idea of paying wages for housework is problematic.[8] To begin with, it could have the effect of validating the idea that women's 'work' is in the home rather than in the wider public sphere. There is also the question of who should pay these 'wages'. The husband? The 'working' spouses in any marriage do, in effect, pay the stay-at-home partners for their domestic labour by taking care of their rent, living expenses and discretionary spending.

Perhaps it is the state that should, in fact, be paying these wages? But this proposition raises the spectre of governments ascribing value to personal relationships. Parenting is not a 'profession' in the same way that accountancy is. Being a mother is a relationship, even though it entails obligations that result in significant amounts of work, just as being a daughter, or a spouse, or a sister-in-law, are all relationships that entail commitment and effort. The thought of the state as arbiter of these relationships is discomfiting.

In fact even in the non-monetarily compensated realm, there is a definite hierarchy of value. Writing books is higher on this scale than raising children. This pecking order can't simply be explained by the fact that authors, unlike 'moms', earn some income, however paltry.

Financially I benefited from Julio's spending on housing, vacations, groceries, domestic help and other expenses over the course of my 'sabbatical' more than what I pulled from my book advance. In other words, Julio had paid me more for being his spouse and caring for our children than I had earned for writing *Punjabi Parmesan.* And yet, it was the latter that gave me some 'worth', or at least that is how I experienced it.

This despite the fact that the time and effort I spent comforting, teaching, dressing, feeding and ferrying the children was valued. Julio valued it, as did the kids' teachers, and, of course, the children themselves. Yet, I felt that the approbation I received for my 'work' as a mother was not enough. I suspect this is what many women experience.

The problem is not that our efforts as homemakers are not valued, but that many of us want to move beyond the domestic realm and generate value in the public sphere as well. Women want the ability to combine different kinds of work, in the private and public spheres, with different kinds of remuneration, monetary and otherwise.

The public and private are not watertight compartments. Private decisions can have public ramifications, just as public policies can influence private choices. Nonetheless, their essential texture is different.

Yet, even in the absence of perfect consonance between the domestic and the public, it is surely possible to work towards solutions that allow individuals to combine and enjoy different kinds of value, to enjoy an amalgamation of choices, rather than the stark work–life non-choice that is the experience of most people today.

Flexibility in work location, part-time work, affordable and high-quality childcare, enforced parental (including paternal) leave, changes in the socialization of children regarding gender norms are all parts of the larger jigsaw puzzle. This puzzle is not 'having it all', but 'having enough'. It's a wonderful puzzle, even if most of us need a lifetime to assemble it and many of us are denied the chance to complete it.

The most exciting post-lay-off development in my life was not the discovery of Georg Simmel (although I like heavy-going, fin de siècle, German philosophy as much as the next person), but Ishaan's burgeoning vocabulary.

As he approached his fourth birthday, my older son remained demanding, obstinate and quite exasperating. Yet, in making the transformation from blob to conversationalist, he was magical. Talking might seem the most mundane of skills, but experiencing a child learning to speak was like watching his brain grow in fast forward. Of course, all this intellectual expansion was quite tricky for a parent to handle.

I began to feel like I needed a doctorate in theology, biology and physics to answer most questions that Ishaan posed. And he posed questions every minute of every day. 'Mama, where does God go to the toilet?' 'Mama, why is a dinosaur not a hippopotamus?' 'Mama, where was I, before I was born?' 'Mama, what is colour?' 'Mama? Mama?'

'Why do you ask so many questions?' I moaned one day, clutching my hair like some comic-book caricature of a mother. Pat came the reply. 'Because I have a mouth,' he said, grinning broadly.

Ishaan always had a ready answer, a comeback. He excelled at repartee, even though most often it was of the nonsensical, three-year-old, variety. I loved it. I found connecting to a child who could verbalize infinitely more absorbing, and rewarding, than bonding with a baby. I loved Ishaan more when he was three than I did when he was an infant. It sounds horrible when written down in black and white. But surely, it's normal to feel more love for someone you've known intimately for several years and with whom you can talk, than for a stranger who erupts into, and disrupts wholly, your life, which is what a baby is, once stripped of the mother–baby mysticism.

Normal or not, it's how I felt with both children. I found my relationship with a baby somewhat adversarial. A baby was something to overcome; something I struggled not to be defeated by. Even Nico, whom I was more prepared for than Ishaan, was not genuinely enjoyable as an infant. He could look very cute, dressed up in striped onesies. And the first time he grabbed my finger gave me an electric shock-like thrill. But for much of his first few months I felt I was performing love rather than experiencing it. What I really wanted from Nico was for him to go to sleep. And I always felt a fluttering sense of release when the nanny came to work, and I could detach from him.

The detaching, however, was never complete. Regardless of whether I was writing the book, travelling or shopping for groceries, the children pervaded my thoughts. I was filled with concerns about their development milestones (Ishaan still couldn't draw intelligible pictures), their diet (Nico ate nothing but rice porridge, raisins and bananas for the first year of his life on solids), their exposure to television (limited, with enormous difficulty, to an hour on the weekends), their temperament (they were both somewhat irascible, like their mother), and their relationship with each other (passionate but fraught).

Ishaan, we discovered, was not an innate nurturer. After his initial scream of anguish upon beholding his baby brother, his main strategy of dealing with Nico had been to ignore him. But as Nico grew older, began to crawl and play with toys, Ishaan became more overtly hostile. He provoked his brother at every opportunity, hiding away the little one's possessions and refusing to respond to friendly overtures. By the time Nico could walk, the two were always pulling and snatching at each other. One of them would start crying within minutes of their cohabiting a space. It was nothing like the rosy picture of contented children playing together that everyone had painted for me when I'd expressed doubts about having a second kid.

Julio's main, rather infuriating, contribution to my tribulations was to tell me to relax. It so happened that he had just read his first parenting book. The paperback was a gift to me from a friend, but it was the title that persuaded my spouse to peruse its contents. The book was titled, *The Idle Parent*, a perfect description of Julio's ultimate parenting ambition.[9] It proposed a laid-back attitude to children, allowing them the space to learn how to organize their own activities. It was certainly funny. And I also took the advice of the author on having an occasional glass of red wine during bath time to make it a more enjoyable affair.

However, much of the book was difficult for me to put into practice. First of all the author, Tom Hodgkinson, was a man who shared the responsibilities of childcare with his spouse in a manner that was quite distinct from the 'he who never left office' husband I had. Moreover, while I quite agreed with the idea that paranoid parents did their children little good, I found reality somewhat different from ideals.

Before I became a mom, I used to agree with theories that suggested parents should not bother about baby-proofing homes, so that children could experience a mild electric shock or two, thus teaching themselves long-lasting lessons in the danger of electric sockets. I also held that rather than trying constantly to keep children healthy, it made more sense to allow them to develop their immune systems by becoming sick. I was, in short, a great advocate of laissez-faire parenting.

Once Ishaan and Nico appeared on the scene, however, I could just as well have taken my former opinions and stuffed them up an orifice. I became as obsessed as every other 'paranoid' mother about their dressing warmly to avoid catching a cold, or washing their hands before eating to reduce the chances of tummy infection. I sterilized pacifiers and brushed every tooth of each child with great care.

Much of this had little to do with worrying about my children getting sick per se. I knew, as much as my pre-mommy self had, that a few colds or stomach bugs were neither wholly avoidable nor a Greek tragedy. In fact, they did boost the immune system. But, the greater problem was the impact even minor illnesses had on *my* life. A cold would mean a sleepless night for me as the baby woke up every half an hour with a blocked nose. A tummy upset equalled unscheduled visits to the doctor and horrible episodes in which I had to force medicine down the throat of a wildly unwilling toddler. My writing deadlines would fall by the wayside. My social plans would unceremoniously be upended. My stress levels would break the gauge.

I had also underestimated the maternal instinct, which had made its presence known to me, despite my ambivalence to many aspects of motherhood. There is something natural about the urge to protect your child. It seemed absurd that I had ever imagined a 'harmless' electric shock to be the best way to teach children about the dangers of sticking their fingers into sockets. The need to protect your kids from pain is as strong as the need to eat and breathe. It is compelling, even when it exhausts you to heed the compulsion. And so Julio's chatter about the virtues of the idle parent did little save raise my blood pressure. The reason my spouse could take the road to idleness was precisely because I didn't.

I was feeling worn out. Even without the pressures of a day job, I never had enough hours in the day. In Europe, the scarcity of labour combined with the high cost of living force people to take on a growing list of roles. One needs to be a mother and plumber and earner of salary and assembler of Ikea furniture. I was even expected to be a supermarket check-out assistant, after our local supermarket equipped all its customers with self-scanning machines with which we needed to tot up our own bills, in the name of efficiency. No wonder my Indian friend had asked me how I had coped 'over here'.

The loss of my salary had knock-on effects. Most of my earnings had gone towards paying our nanny. I no longer had an income, but I could not do without her assistance. It was difficult to justify when I couldn't afford it, but I was aware that if I relinquished help at home, I would also be giving up any hope of a life beyond the domestic. It would spell a farewell to *Punjabi Parmesan*, an adios to lay-off as opportunity to reflect and recharge. The nanny stayed. My bank account shrank. It rained almost every day, as was the predilection of Belgian weather.

And then, one early spring evening, Julio asked how I would feel about moving to tropical Indonesia. All those justifications about the opportunities to which his current workaholic job would lead had proved accurate. Despite having less experience than was the norm for a position in an EU delegation abroad, Julio had successfully applied for a post in Indonesia.

At first I didn't know what to think. Our goal throughout had been to try and move to India next, so that we could be closer to my family, and give the children a chance to learn more about their Indian heritage. Indonesia shared a similar-sounding name to India, but it was not somewhere that had loomed large on my mental cartography.

I knew it was a populous, Muslim-majority country and I had an imprecise hunch that it was probably more important than was internationally acknowledged. It had a fast-growing economy and was often touted as a democratic success story. Moreover, the archipelago shared historical and civilizational links with India that had been forgotten about in contemporary times. The more I thought about it the more excited I began to feel. Indonesia certainly promised to be more adventurous journalistically than Europe, a continent that managed to be somewhat dull even in the midst of a crisis.

Then there were all the practical considerations. We would have a generous housing allowance. Our euros would go a lot further when converted to rupiah in Indonesia. A nanny would no longer stretch our finances quite as much. I would have more time to focus on writing *Punjabi Parmesan*. Our kids could learn Mandarin at school. We could Skype with my mother more easily given the inconsequential time difference. And I would no longer have to check out my own groceries.

I recalled all the foot massages and aromatic body rubs that tourism promotion videos on South-East Asia featured. And momentarily high on the imagined scent of frangipani, I agreed. 'Let's go to Indonesia, darling,' I said, smiling at Julio.

7

TOUCH

AUGUST 2012–13

Moving to a new country with two boys under the age of five can feel cataclysmic. We touched down in Jakarta late on a Saturday evening after an epic twenty-hour series of flights that left us unmoored. Our bodies were out of sync with our minds, as time zones were crossed, and senses dulled by the nowhere-everywhere-ness of airports and planes.

The drive to our cramped, temporary accommodation was interminable. En route we dropped off the cats at the quarantine centre where Indonesian law required them to spend two weeks. It was bumper-to-bumper traffic virtually the entire way into the city centre. Nico flopped about in the car and Ishaan chattered away, asking rapid-fire questions that made my head hurt. I slipped Nico a steady stream of M&Ms to settle him, and snapped at Ishaan to be quiet, covering myself in parenting glory all around.

The next day I was dazed and frightened. What had I agreed to? Nico had been up the whole night and I'd passed the hours walking him up and down the short corridor of the flat until we'd both passed out on the living-room sofa, just as the call of the azan, heralding the morning prayer, wafted through the closed windows.

The unfamiliarity of our surroundings when combined with the exhaustion was almost hallucinogenic. The heat was a heavy presence; the unruly traffic, jarring. We tried going for a walk but discovered Jakarta's pavements, where they existed, were not designed with strollers in mind. We navigated through gaping potholes, sewer rats and mounds of garbage. We found a McDonalds and bought a spicy chicken burger from a headscarved saleswoman.

I felt like a character out of a Conrad novel disembarking on to the docks of a confusing humid city in the East Indies. The irony of someone from India (who had also lived in China) reacting in this manner wasn't lost on me. Even allowing for reverse culture shock, I was aware that however chaotic, polluted and traffic-clogged Indonesia was, India was more so, of everything.

But in India I was protected by family and the invisible but elaborate network of systems and privileges this afforded me. I was able to live a fairly interior life, cocooned from the monstrous, realities of the outside. Air-conditioned cars, security-guard-monitored neighbourhoods and a certain attitude of not seeing the unlovely – a common condition afflicting the elite – combined to keep me removed from the public experience of life. In Indonesia, I had no such protection. And coming after over three years in pretty, chocolate-scented Brussels, everything about Jakarta seemed off kilter.

For the next few months it was as though I were living on top of, rather than inside of, Indonesia, skidding across its slippery surface instead of sinking my claws into its substantial interior. My days were filled with ferrying Ishaan to his new school, managing the help, taking Nico to 'mommy and me' classes, where I was compelled to sing nursery rhymes with exaggerated enunciation, and meeting other expat mothers.

My life narrowed to the banal domestic. For the first time, people addressed me as Madam or Mrs. I had to enter 'housewife' on the immigration form, there being no option for the unemployed freethinking intellectual category I would have preferred. I was soon running a small and medium enterprise called home, supervising 'staff' and repairs.

Indonesia's intriguing politics, not to mention its white-sand beaches, beckoned alluringly, but remained frustratingly beyond my baby-holding grasp. I managed to sneak in a couple of hours working on the Europe book every morning but the bulk of the day disappeared in dealing with the problems of the privileged in developing countries. Our water pipes regularly attempted to end their old and rusty lives. But our fabulously rich landlord was resolute in his opposition to putting them out of their misery and instead instructed his plumbing minions to extract every last minute of life still left in them. Regular water stoppages resulted from these badly executed patch jobs. Luckily, although there was often no water in the toilets or taps, we were able to flush and mop by using buckets of swimming pool water.

In the afternoons I took Ishaan to after-school activities: swimming, gymnastics, art. I carted my laptop along and occasionally managed a paragraph or two of writing, but mostly ended up in repetitive conversations with other moms about what my husband did in Jakarta, where I bought my groceries, which other classes I planned to sign my kids up for, and how difficult it was to find reliable nannies.

Despite the limited opportunities I had for expanding my horizons beyond the personal I caught glimpses of something fascinating every day, like the scattered pieces of a puzzle that I only put together in later, more reflective, months. Scanning the newspapers revealed a smorgasbord of improbable monikers: Teddy Anwar, Wisnu Ali, Veronica Colondam, Leanardus Nyoman, Goenawan Mohammad. The syncretism of the names was intriguing. The architectural equivalents of these names also reared up ever so often. An enormous statue of the Hindu god Krishna, leading the Pandava prince Arjuna into battle, stood to the south-west of Monas, the country's main nationalist monument. Diagonally across, the marble minaret of Jakarta's largest mosque, the Istiqlal, and the cast-iron steeples of the city's Catholic Cathedral, jointly punctuated the skyline.

Once my initial disorientation had worn off, Indonesia began to appear familiar in a way that China never had. For most Indians, Beijing was alienating. The Chinese language was opaque in sight and sound. The scale of Chinese imperial palaces and their communist equivalents could feel outlandish, the highways impossibly smooth and the winter cold frighteningly desolate. Despite the fact that the days when everyone dressed in identical Mao suits were long over, there was an underlying uniformity to the physical and intellectual lives of Chinese cities that was discomfiting. The heated political debates that were par for the course on Indian trains were absent. The pageantry of street demonstrations and strikes was missing. Calls to prayer and the ringing of temple bells were rarely part of the aural backdrop.

But in Jakarta, the timbre of everyday life was distinctly Indian. Regular demonstrations by everyone from workers clamouring for higher minimum wage to religious hardliners demanding the cancellation of Lady Gaga concerts caused massive gridlock on the roads; little retail shops selling every imaginable good from talcum powder to chocolate remained sheltered in the shade of extravagant malls; the call of muezzins punctuated the day; the warmth of petrichor hung over gardens and women in burkhas shopped in stores assisted by mini-skirted sales staff.

Many Indonesian islands, including the most populous one,

Java, had been ruled by Hindu and Buddhist kings for centuries, before the region converted to Islam over the sixteenth and seventeenth centuries. Hindu cultural norms continued to infuse indigenous mores. Everywhere – embedded in the language, on street signs, political commentary and bus advertisements – I found references to the Hindu epics, the Ramayana and the Mahabharata. My local mechanic was called Rama Repairs. I discovered a nationwide charitable foundation for twins called the Nakula and Sadewa Society. Buses were painted with large advertisements for an energy drink called Kuku Bima, which promised the imbiber Bhima-like endurance.

Indonesia was clearly India's South-East Asian doppelgänger: democratic, youthful, dynamic, diverse and corrupt. And this is how I eventually pitched the idea of my reporting from Jakarta to the newspaper I formerly wrote for from China. The editor was receptive and quick to offer me a job as Indonesia correspondent. The offer, however, was accompanied by yet another pay cut. Inured as I was by this time to the downward trajectory of my earnings, I agreed without much of a fight. The global economic outlook and the Indian media job market were both gloomy. And, as before, a lower salary went some way to assuage imagined future guilt associated with the flexibility that parenting required.

Despite the extra help I now had at home I found the days vanishing under the crush of memsahib-ish to-do lists. International schools in Asia seemed to function on the assumption that either mothers did not work, or had a platoon of nannies to assist them. In many cases, both scenarios held. One Gucci-wearing mom at Ishaan's school screamed in mock horror when I told her that I had two boys under five. 'Soooo tough! When my boys were that age, I was just deeead,' she said. 'I used to have five or six nannies all around me. The work was simply non-stop.'

Ishaan's school let out at 12.30 in the afternoon and day-care centre for preschoolers did not appear to exist in the Indonesian capital (that's what nannies were for). The only available options to keep fifteen-month-old Nico occupied were hour-long mommy-and-me classes. Luckily, the nanny I eventually employed, was able to look after Nico at home for much of the day. But it was soon clear that she was not optimal company for Ishaan. My four-year-old was beyond the stage when someone without multiple advanced university degrees could meet his needs.

Our Indonesian nanny spoke only broken English and was rarely able to understand his questions – 'Why don't numbers end?', 'What is beyond Pluto?', 'When will I pass away?' – leave alone provide adequate responses. Ishaan was also too bossy to be disciplined in any meaningful manner by this easy-going, mild-mannered lady.

I was grappling with the unanticipated situation of being needed by my child more, as he grew older. I had imagined the baby stage to be the most consuming of a mother's time. It is the first few months of a child's life when women take time off work. And so much feminist effort is expended on fighting for longer maternity leave, with arguments about breastfeeding taking centre stage. I'd assumed that the older and more independent a child became, the easier it would be to achieve work–life balance. But I was finding it harder.

Ishaan the baby had needed to be diapered and rocked. But Ishaan the boy argued and negotiated. He wondered and theorized. He fought with his brother and needed someone to practise his reading with. He was essentially morphing into a vacuum cleaner set on sucking up Mama's day.

It was round about this time that I read former senior US State Department official Anne Marie Slaughter's article in *The Atlantic* magazine about how she had found it impossible to juggle a high-powered government job in foreign policy with bringing up her two teenage boys.[1] Yikes! If I was finding it difficult with a two- and-four-year-old, how was I going to manage when Ishaan and Nico were in their teens? By then they would be able to use the toilet and fix their own meals – one hoped – but what about their drug problems, mood swings and anarchic beliefs? It was a chilling thought.

I willed myself not to panic. Motherhood is a long-haul journey and it is best to take it one unexpected learning at a time. I decided to defer my job offer for a while. The newspaper editor agreed to wait until I was ready. Historical ties and contemporary similarities notwithstanding, the archipelago ranked even below Europe on the Indian editorial agenda. I was determined to change this misguided state of affairs. But I needed to bide my time. There were bylines, but there were also babies. And, as always, there were hard choices to be made.

Nico clung to me like a limpet in those first few months in Jakarta. I was his sole preoccupation. He wasn't even interested in TV. I'd survived Ishaan's terrible twos thanks to Baby Einstein videos, and Disney's infernal, *Cars.* Ishaan would sit glued to the screen, momentarily zombified, and mercifully still, whenever I played these for him. But TV didn't seem to register in Nico's brain; he simply didn't 'see' the screen. His eyes were permanently fixed on his mother.

More than Ishaan, more than anyone, including my husband, Nico needed to touch me. He went to sleep cupping my cheeks with his little hands. He held hands with me while eating his breakfast. That boys and mothers have a special bond is received wisdom, but there was a physical intensity to that relationship that I had not expected.

The ghost of Oedipus stalked the corridors of our home. Ishaan insisted (until he was six) that he would marry me once he grew up. Whenever I reminded him, gently, that I was already married to Papa, he retorted dismissively, 'I'm not saying we'll get married now. I mean later.' That Papa would mysteriously exit the scene 'later' was implicit.

As Nico grew, and finally began to expand his diet beyond raisins, his body became plump and fragrant like a peach. Unlike Ishaan who was too squirmy to be much of a cuddler, Nico was sensual. His stroking was feathery, his eye contact smouldering. His precise kissing caused nerve-tingling ecstasy to the recipient of the kiss. By the time he had become obsessed with *Star Wars*, which, thanks to older brother Ishaan, was astonishingly soon, Nico declared himself to be a Jedi dedicated to protecting Princess Padme, aka mama.

All my feminist principles evaporated. I shamelessly begged him for protection and simpered in delight when he wrapped his soft arms around me while warding off imaginary attackers. Julio was jealous. Not of me, but Nico. He wanted to be the 'princess' who Nico wanted to look after. 'Help me, Jedi!' he implored Nico. 'Hug me or else General Grevious will eat me.'

These are natural phases that children (and parents) go through and they felt very natural. Touching my boys and being touched by them was wholesome, even healing. A juicy kiss was the best apology my kids could give me. Spooning them at night was more effective than any lullaby at lulling them to sleep. A hug was superior to medicine for a bruised knee or hurting heart.

And yet having children reframed the experience of the body and intimacy. In adult life the body is either the focus of modesty, involving its clothing and shielding from the public gaze, or of eroticism, involving disrobing and the private gaze of a lover. For me, intimate touch had long equalled an erotic touch.

Having children changed this equivalence. My boys were from my body and of my body. They had fed from my body. They felt like extensions of my body. Their touch was intimate, lingering, pleasurable yet non-erogenous.

Growing up in India, nudity was restricted to bath time and occurred behind locked doors. I cannot recall ever seeing either of my parents naked. Middle-class Indian homes are not private. They heave with people. Maids and odd-job men wander around. Neighbours drop by without announcement. Stray aunts lurk in corners.

My childhood home had been no exception. Even our grandfather had lived with us until he passed away, by which time I was at university. So had the two nurses who worked twelve-hour shifts and provided him with the round-the-clock care his Alzheimer's disease necessitated. Everyone was always clothed.

So, even though I was aware of comparatively liberal attitudes in northern Europe, when a Danish friend at Oxford revealed that it was normal for his parents to traipse around naked at home in front of him, I was truly scandalized. It sounded entirely inappropriate, even a tad pornographic.

And yet, now that the warm weather in Indonesia permitted it, it wasn't rare for my kids to catch me in my birthday suit. The word 'catch' isn't quite accurate given how it implies something illicit or at least unusual. But, for them it was as normal to see me in the nude post-shower, blow-drying my hair, as it was for them to see each other naked in the bath. We didn't have live-in help or unexpected relatives, and the house was often empty save for the kids and me. Bathroom doors were never locked and the kids traipsed in and out quite obliviously.

I hadn't set out to achieve some kind of nudist ideal. There was just so much of the body, naked skin, and touch involved when Ishaan and Nico were infants that we had simply carried on, as a family, from there. Once when Nico was around three, I decided it was finally time to lock the door while I did my business. But almost as soon as I sat down on the throne armed with a cup of tea and a copy of the *Jakarta Post*, Nico began hammering to be let in. 'Go away and play. I want some privacy, darling,' I shouted out. 'So do I, mama,' he replied. 'I want some privacy with you.'

The boys talked about my breasts occasionally. They called them *tetas*, the informal Spanish term for mammaries. Once as we walked past the lingerie section in a Jakarta department store, Ishaan pointed at the lacy bras on display and loudly asked me to 'look at all the teta holders'. Another time I caught Nico trying to breastfeed his teddy bear. 'If I eat a lot of spinach will my tetas become big like yours?' he asked.

I found moments like these hilarious. But sometimes I experienced fleeting self-doubt. Was I bringing up perverts? Had I crossed a line? Touch is the first language mother and child use to communicate, but not all touch is equal.

A major scandal broke out at one of the top international schools in Jakarta, during our second year in Indonesia. A group of janitors and two teachers were accused of sexually molesting a kindergartener and subsequently arrested.[2] Schools across the city responded by holding seminars to educate children on the difference between 'good' touch and 'bad' touch.

Ishaan came home after one of these and announced that his private parts were his business alone. I nodded my approval. 'No one should ever touch them,' he continued, 'except parents and teachers.' I nearly choked. 'I think you mean parents and doctors, darling,' I corrected. 'Oh ya,' he said distractedly, by now more focused on his latest Lego creation, 'that's what I meant.'

In the end I needn't have worried. As he grew older, Ishaan stopped wanting to hang around me when I was in the shower or getting dressed. If he walked in on me inadvertently, he averted his eyes and muttered 'sorry'. The temperature of the touch we shared altered. It cooled. The tempo changed. Hugs became quicker. Kisses more fleeting. His body elongated.

Nico, who always took cues from his brother, also made stabs at developing modesty. He took to putting his hands over his eyes when I emerged from the shower. But because he was only a little fellow who loved his mother's company, his fingers would invariably part a moment or two later as he began recounting the heroic exploits of Jedi knight Nico Wan Kanobi.

The days drifted into a rhythm. I worked on *Punjabi Parmesan* in the morning and hung out with the children in the afternoon. I even managed the occasional byline, reviewing books. On Wednesdays I went to the local spa for a foot massage. The cats (who had survived their quarantine period unscathed) scratched our furniture and flopped about in the tropical heat. Julio was usually home by the kids' bedtime (although this did not necessarily translate into him putting them to bed).

My return to weekly reflexology after almost four years in damp, labour-scarce, expensive and lethargic Brussels was indicative of how good it was to be back in warm, dynamic, affordable Asia. But as this description itself indicates, many of these benefits were predicated on deep inequality.

On our morning drive to school in CD-plated, seven-seat car splendour, bedraggled children hawking flowers or begging for money surrounded us at traffic lights. For the first time in his conscious life Ishaan experienced the frightening, cruel reality of an arbitrarily segregated society, where an undeserved twist of fate decides whether you sleep in a five-bedroom villa or next to an open sewer.

I had grown up amongst such inequality, but seeing it through my son's eyes made it impossible to ignore. 'Why are those children on the road by themselves? It's dangerous. Where are their parents?' he would ask, no doubt recalling the numerous times I'd insisted he hold my hand when we crossed a street. On spotting a ten-year-old, sad-eyed busker, 'Look at that girl with the guitar. How cool! Can I get a guitar?'

I had no happy answers. 'They're alone because they are poor.' 'Why are they poor?' 'Because they are unlucky.' 'What is unlucky?' Hating my answer, but saying it nonetheless: 'When you don't have any money.'

Even within the plush malls that dotted Jakarta there was no respite from Ishaan's uncomfortable gaze. Young women, some of whom looked no older than sixteen or seventeen, wearing the white tunics and shorts that were the standard uniform for pembantus, as nannies are called in Indonesia, trailed after designer-outfit-draped memsahibs, carrying the latter's offspring in slings. They fed these fat-cheeked infants with bottles, cradled them when they fussed, and wiped the spittle off their chins. The mothers shopped.

These girls were ordered around, yet rarely seen by their employers. But Ishaan saw them. 'Why is that mom carrying a baby in that thing?' he asked, indicating a sling. 'She's not the baby's mom, darling,' I replied. 'How do you know?' he asked. 'She's too young,' I ventured. 'That's the mom,' pointing to the blow-dried beauty sashaying ahead of the nanny. 'Why isn't the mom holding the baby?' 'Because it hurts her arms.' 'Doesn't it hurt the nanny's arms?' 'Probably, but it's her job.' 'What do you mean?' 'She's paid to do it.' 'What is "paid"?'

I had spent much time talking to Ishaan about concepts like 'fair play' and 'justice'. But I was at a loss to explain injustice as fact, especially given that we were the beneficiaries of this deeply unfair world. On Ishaan's fifth birthday a friend gave us a picture-book version of Charles Dickens's *A Tale of Two Cities.* It began with the French revolution. 'What is revolution?' he immediately asked. I tried my best to explain the huge gulf between the rich and poor in seventeenth-century France that had caused the peasantry to rise up against the aristocracy.

'So the poor killed the rich in the revolution?' asked Ishaan, his eyes as large as footballs. Then apprehensively: 'Will there be a revolution in Indonesia also?' Ishaan obviously identified with the 'rich'. He was nervous of the 'poor'. It was a reaction that upset me.

I am Indian. I come from a poor country. I did not want to bring up a coddled First-World child in whom poverty provoked anxiety or distaste. Most of all I didn't want my children to feel the kind of indifference that was common amongst elites in developing countries. I knew how easily inequality becomes banal. How quickly poverty is accepted and then scarcely noticed.

I wanted my boys to have empathy for the poor. To feel angry at the grotesque injustices they suffer. To understand how privilege protects and perpetuates itself. I wanted them to want to heal the world. But I also wanted them to enjoy the material comforts of the well off. To build sand castles on a beach in Bali. To learn Mandarin and circus skills. To have the best medical care, and to sleep under a fluffy duvet. This was an inconsistent position, and I knew it. But that's how it was.

In the upper-crust, English–Chinese bilingual school that Ishaan and Nico went to, efforts were made at 'community outreach'. The school worked with an organization called Kampung Kids and every year parents donated some money to the outfit and were asked to persuade their children to part with a few toys as well. *Kampung* translates as village, although in an urban context it could also refer to slum.

The idea of teaching the kids about 'charity' was distasteful to me. There was a whiff of smugness in the manner in which the children were told how fortunate they were. It was as if they were already being groomed as elites belonging to a charmed circle, who occasionally chucked a couple of toys down from the high table to the grateful unwashed masses as an easy massage for their collective conscience.

Yet, I struggled to do any better myself, falling back on the lame platitudes of parents everywhere, telling the boys how lucky they were to have a choice of chicken curry and spaghetti for lunch. 'Don't you know that there are kids who are starving?'

I tried to prevent the kids from taking our advantages for granted by repeating versions of the snore-inducing stories my father had regaled my brother and me with about his deprived childhood. 'I got my first wristwatch when I was at university,' Papa had told me while reluctantly presenting me with my own cheap model at the age of fifteen – years after the majority of my classmates had owned one. 'I got my first watch at the age of fifteen,' I found myself telling Ishaan dolorously as I handed him his first plastic, Mickey-mouse-decorated wristwatch on his fifth birthday.

In response, Ishaan rolled his eyes at me like a teenager. Nico cupped my chin and whispered sultrily, 'It's OK, Padme. Don't be sad.'

As the months became years, Ishaan stopped confusing nannies with moms. And he stopped asking about why there were unaccompanied children selling flowers at traffic lights. 'Oh, that's just a kampong kid,' he might say if asked. That short, dismissive sentence felt like a slap in the face.

Jakarta marked my first encounter with the infamous Tiger Mom. Founded by one of Indonesia's most wealthy Chinese families, the children's school was the hunting grounds of diamond-dripping Asian mothers with big ambitions for their children. The founder's daughter, a moon-faced child with a perpetually worried look, was Ishaan's classmate.

This four-year-old began her mornings an hour earlier than the other children with a wushu class. By the time she was five, she was taking part in international martial art competitions. The child was polite and seemingly uncomplaining. Her handwriting was beautiful and her artwork always pinned up on the classroom display board for its neat and pleasing aesthetics. In a corridor conversation her mother told me that she was training her daughter to *kowtow* to her in traditional Chinese style. 'I think it instills respect. Don't you?' she asked me mildly, leaving my head spinning in a million directions as I thought of Ishaan's epic sassiness.

Just the other day he'd asked why I could watch TV every evening when he was only allowed to on the weekends. 'Because I'm your mother and I can do whatever I want,' I had declared hoping, without much hope, that the resounding tone of my delivery would staunch further remark. 'Oh?' Ishaan had countered, unfazed. 'Can you climb a tree with no branches? Or cut down a coconut? Or make a sphere into a cube?' (Who knew that a kindergarten discussion on 'shapes' could be wielded against a hapless mother thus?)

Unfortunately (for Ishaan), my encounters at his school coincided with my finally reading Amy Chua's *Battle Hymn of the Tiger Mother*, the book responsible for popularizing the concept of the achievement-focused, no-nonsense parenting style that was apparently the predilection of 'Asian' parents.

I had an inkling of the cultural context of Tiger Parenting having gone through the Indian school system. My mother had been a busy, working mom who had left me to my own devices with access to a vast library and not much else. But the kind of school I went to, typical of India, was almost wholly focused on academics, with reams of homework and constant examinations that required copious by-rote memorization and regurgitation.

My alma mater had been a stereotypical Tiger compared to the fluffy Bunny that is the average American-influenced international school, with its emphasis on art and craft, learning as fun, building self-esteem and encouraging self-expression.

The kids' school was a confused Tiger–Bunny hybrid that attempted to fuse the Chinese and American models, and left me equally befuddled in the process. Chinese class was full of hard-core memorization and copying out of characters. But the rest of the day consisted of time with Western faculty who cooked spaghetti for the 'Science' lesson, and insisted children not be 'forced' to write. I was told by Ishaan's homeroom teacher to make sure I never used lined paper, a staple of my own childhood, when encouraging him to write.

'Give him a large empty sheet, a pencil and just let the child experiment.' When I replied that this strategy only produced a mess of barely identifiable, asymmetrical squiggles, the teacher held up a hand to shush me. 'That's normal,' he said and I acquiesced, although I couldn't help sneaking a wistful peek at the carefully etched 'essays' pinned on the display board that some of Ishaan's classmates, notably the kowtowing wushu warrior, had produced.

The Tiger–Bunny duality of the school posed a conundrum that I managed with avoidance. I sublimated all thoughts that Ishaan was lagging behind, whenever they reared their ugly heads. Between answering his infinite stock of questions and writing *Punjabi Parmesan* there was little time to worry too much. And the fact that my mother had been a pretty laissez-faire parent helped affirm my chosen strategy. I'd turned out fine – or so I like to think.

Then came the day I picked up Amy Chua's *Battle Hymn.* By the time I was through the first couple of chapters it was as if the third eye of Shiva had awoken within me. Some dormant genetic strain of Asian momhood kicked into gear and began roaring instructions in my ear that were impossible to ignore.

Amy Chua had ensured that her daughter was an accomplished

pianist by the age of six, obediently practising her scales for *hours* every day. Her children were 'polite, interesting, helpful and well-spoken'. They were fluent in Mandarin. They did not go on play dates because they spent their 'free' time perfecting various intricate competencies.

She explained that it was not as if her daughters hadn't resisted her draconian demands. But she did not let complaints, tears, or even tantrums deter her, because children always oppose learning a difficult new skill at the beginning when they are not very good at it. Chua pointed out that this was where Western parents tended to give up.

But by persisting even in the face of vehement opposition from the child, 'Asian' parents create a virtuous circle wherein eventually a child begins to excel at the task at hand and therefore to enjoy it. The child attracts praise and this builds their confidence and appetite for further hard work. By forcing their children not to surrender, 'Asian' mothers signal to their children that they trust in their ability to rise to a difficult challenge. By caving in to a child's protestations they only set them up for further failure.

I was mortified. I had been a terrible mother to Ishaan, signalling to him that I did not believe he could do better than squiggles on a large, blank sheet of paper. If only I had trusted him more, it would be his work displayed on the classroom board and his name appearing in Wushu competitions.

I needed to find my stripes. Amy Chua had kept her daughters up until midnight perfecting their Chinese characters, but I heaped Ishaan with praise if he merely managed a relatively undrunken *heng* or *shu* (the most basic horizontal and vertical strokes). The first time my son had put his head underwater at swimming class, I had leapt up and down clapping in encouragement and later bought him a vanilla milkshake in reward. Amy Chua would have spat on him, called him 'garbage' and refused to feed him at all until he had mastered the butterfly stroke. I spent hours supervising play dates (mostly in the hope of reciprocity, so that I could occasionally be rid of Ishaan on no-school days). Amy Chua did not believe in friends. Time spent socializing was time away from maths, Mandarin and classical music.

When I looked at it with Amy Chua's Tiger eyes, it became clear that Ishaan was basically useless. He often coloured outside the margins in drawing class. By the time he managed to do up the buttons of his shirt, Amy Chua's daughter would have performed a dazzling Mozart concerto. He was not the most coordinated of children and fumbled catching a ball.

None of this was the problem. I was. I had been craven in not insisting on perfection. I had let him down by not practising 'catch' for ten hours straight, if this is what was needed to improve his hand-to-eye coordination. I had been a bad mother for doing up his buttons for him when he was late for school instead of waking up half an hour earlier to make sure he had enough time to do the buttons again, and again, if necessary. I vowed to mend my ways immediately.

For the next month I sat down with Ishaan at a desk for hours after school, forcing him to write legible letters. When he failed, I told him to try again, repeating that I believed he could do it if he only tried harder. I kept calm. For the first hour or so. But eventually I would lose it and start yelling. 'Why can't you just write the damn "p"?' I shouted and gnashed my teeth at his incompetence. After he failed to write a word with even-sized letters over the course of an entire afternoon, I gripped his shoulder so hard he winced and announced we would not get up until he produced results.

Touch is not only playful, nurturing or sexual. It can be hard. And can hurt. I can't really put a gloss on this, so here is what happened: I smacked Ishaan. Multiple times. There were occasions when I asked him to put out his hand and slapped it in a calculated manner when other attempts at enforcing discipline had failed. But more often it was because I lost my temper. As a reaction rather than a controlled decision.

The impact on Ishaan appeared to be short-lived. He'd wilt for a moment or two but yo-yoed back to his cheeky self with great resilience. The impact on me lasted longer. I didn't feel good about it. No sane parent would. However, I didn't feel completely undone by it either. On the hierarchy of guilt, the failure to breastfeed had ranked higher than the occasional whack.

In my childhood, physical punishment had been like the buzz of mosquitoes, an unwelcome but unremarkable part of the mundane background. My mother spanked me when I was naughty. I bore it with reasonable cheer and it didn't stop me from flushing my spinach down the toilet when she wasn't looking. Teachers at school smacked kids when they misbehaved. It didn't stop us from whispering with our friends instead of listening to their tedious explanations of past participles.

Once, I played truant from sports class in Grade 3 and made off for the playground instead. When found out I was made to crawl around the sports field as punishment. My knees were scratched up by the end of the ordeal, but I was mostly relieved that the teacher didn't send home a note for my mother. Then I would have been in *real* trouble.

There was a deranged maths teacher in middle school who threw thumbscrew compasses used for drawing circles in geometry at students who were not paying attention. Could I be remembering this correctly? Could teachers really have thrown spiked metallic objects at students at the elite public school I attended in New Delhi? I am reasonably sure that my memory is accurate, although we are talking about 1988. I remember my friends and I as simultaneously horrified and impressed by the teacher in question. His precision was legendary. The compasses invariably landed on students' desks rather than their bodies.

What I know to be beyond dispute was the morning assembly ritual in which the school principal personally slapped every male child caught transgressing rules, in front of the entire school. The principal gathered himself up and then really leant in, bringing the full weight of his robust body to bear, as his hand landed on the hapless boy's cheek. Girls were spared this public beating. My school had been sexist and violent. Not that I'd noticed it particularly.

I had enjoyed school, insisting I was well even when sick, so as not to miss out on a single day. And I had adored my mother, completely and without reservation. It never occurred to me, even in passing, that I was abused as a child. And I still cannot countenance the theory that I was. I was smacked, slapped and, once, made to crawl around the schoolyard on my knees. But I had felt wholly emotionally secure, physically safe and intellectually encouraged.

So it was bewildering when I first encountered the idea that parents should (and in some countries could) be criminally prosecuted for smacking their kids. A Swedish friend from my Beijing days had been insistent that a parent who hit a child warranted jail. But surely there is a line between parental discipline and abuse? Between a smack and a punch? Or is there? How much of a slippery slope is there in making such distinctions? What does it take to transform the parent who occasionally spanks a child with the aim to discipline, or even in frustration, into a monster who causes lasting damage, emotional or physical, to their child?

My mother had not slipped down any such slope. The thought of her being jailed on account of me was incomprehensible. She had been the person who had kissed and made life better. She had soothed and listened, laughed and tickled. She had worked relentlessly to pay the rent. She had encouraged me to reach high.

I cannot think of a better role model. As a child, I had not feared her and nor had I resented her.

She was far from perfect. She might have lashed out at me once in a while, verbally and physically. She hadn't breastfed me, as I discovered. But, perfection is not required by children. Love, in all its complexity, is. And she gave me that in spades.

Child-rearing practices vary over geography, culture and time. On the whole, parenting is far more restrictive today than it was a generation ago. When I was growing up I was allowed to play unsupervised with the neighbourhood children. Car seats did not exist. The only concern over my drinking sugary sodas was financial, not health-related. Our family folklore is full of stories of cousins nearly getting electrocuted at weddings or almost drowning in lakes on vacations. These vignettes provoke much mirth and everyone chuckles recalling the good old times.

In contrast, Ishaan and Nico are watched hawk-like by an adult at all times. They are not allowed into our garden unless lathered in mosquito repellent and sunscreen. They are strapped into car seats, though on a good day a centipede could probably crawl faster than the traffic in Jakarta. They are denied sodas on account of low nutritional value and excessive sugar.

I am not blindly repeating the childcare practices of my youth with my own kids. The world has changed, as it does with every generational spin of the cosmic wheel. There are new and different challenges confronting parents. There are new and increasing amounts of information available. I have read and absorbed much contemporary parenting advice. Consequently, there is much that I have done differently with my children.

I also don't believe in smacking children because I was spanked to no ill effect myself. A more sensitive child than I had been, or a more cruel parent than my mother was, would render my personal experience irrelevant. Hitting a child is not a good disciplinary tactic. It may achieve short-term compliance, but long-term changes in behaviour require patient teaching, not quick-tempered smacking. Asking children not to react to frustrations physically, by hitting their siblings or friends, when spanking them yourself, is undoubtedly hypocritical.[3] Moreover, it usually leaves the parent concerned wracked with remorse. Spanking is a lose-lose strategy.

So why did I smack Ishaan? I suppose my own childhood had some role to play in it. But it was also because of my temperament – volatile. And my child's – pig-headed and disobedient. These are not excuses. They are explanations that do not excuse. I am ashamed that I ever raised my hand at Ishaan. I truly wish I never had.

But do I fear I have scarred my child for life? Not really. At least not on account of spanking. Studies, like a recent one by researchers at the Albert Einstein College of Medicine in New York, published in the journal *Parenting: Science and Practice*, found that a child's feeling of being loved offsets the negative effects of 'harsh discipline' like spanking.[4] I don't really need studies to tell me this. Ishaan is enough proof on his own.

'Why do birds fly?' he asked me one Saturday morning. 'Because they have wings,' I replied perfunctorily. 'I have wings too,' he said. I looked up, interested. 'Really? I can't see them. Where are they?' 'Oh, they're just resting, folded on my belly,' Ishaan said, smiling, mischief dancing in his eyes. My son was not scarred.

Nico managed to avoid being spanked or 'Tiger-mommized'. Such is the luck of the second child. I was so much more indulgent a parent when it came to the little one. When Nico mixed up his Bs and Ds or wrote 'S' backwards for the tenth time in a row, I merely responded with a fond, 'silly little monkey'. To which he'd pout and say, 'I'm not a monkey. I'm a person.' And then I'd kiss him. A lot.

I didn't expect Nico to be smart or developmentally advanced. I wanted him to stay a baby for as long as he could, for Ishaan had shown me how fleeting the dimpled cuteness of toddlerdom is. Nico was also more emotionally attuned, and therefore manipulative, than his older brother. Where Ishaan would argue till the fat lady sang (or his old lady gave him a smack), Nico yielded the moment he realized he'd gone too far. And in any case, by the time he was old enough to be doing anything more complicated than colouring, I had abandoned 'Tiger-momming' altogether.

Even Ishaan had to put up with my Amy Chua–inspired claws for only a few months. At some point Shiva's third eye turned inward and the stupidity of my behaviour emerged from the fog of misguided ambition for my child. Ishaan was a curious and confident young person whom I had in effect been undermining, rather than encouraging. He was not Amy Chua's child. He was not the kowtowing-enthusiast's son. He was mine. And I needed to embrace that beautiful simplicity. I resolved never to spank him again.

By the time Ishaan was six his handwriting was acceptable, if not quite of calligraphic merit. He could do up his buttons quickly enough – although they were often misaligned. I moved him to a new school where he was awarded a merit certificate for 'asking a brilliant question during the unit of inquiry'. He'd asked his teacher whether it was possible to have a different age on the outside and inside. 'You might be quite old on the outside but feel young on the inside,' he said. When the teacher nodded approvingly, Ishaan continued, 'Or you could be like me. I am six on the outside, but ten on the inside.'

My son was wise, funny and argumentative. But although I'd abandoned any form of physical discipline, he still drove me to distraction. When stripped down, parenting sounds so simple. It is only about avoiding excess, and developing the confidence to listen to one's intuition. You merely have to encourage and leave alone; to restrain and indulge; to add a bit of this and take away a dash of that; to be open to altering the recipe according to the personality of the child. But it is not simple. Sometimes, it is harder than walking on hot coals.

As the *Punjabi Parmesan* manuscript approached completion, Julio made increasingly pushy suggestions about my returning to 'work'. We'd been living in Indonesia for a year and were past settling in. We had made some friends and decided on a favourite restaurant. Our container of furniture from Brussels had long arrived. The children had predictable routines with school, playgroups and afternoon activities.

In theory I agreed with Julio. It was time. It was ridiculous to have barely engaged with the country we lived in, beyond grocery shopping and home maintenance. I also wanted a proper salary again. Nonetheless, I flew off the handle when Julio suggested that I think about generating an income stream of my own again. I accused him of being ungrateful for all the work I did around the house; for the time and effort I invested in the children. I felt undermined. And I was angry at his apparent resentment at having to share his earnings with his self-sacrificing spouse.

Julio weathered the storm of my response with some grace. He explained that it was not the money that motivated his suggestion. He was unhappily aware that compensation packages for journalists were not going to enable him to retire in comfort. But he did not believe someone with my ability and qualifications should 'just' be a mother. He wanted me to have a public platform for my opinions. His urging me to get a 'job' stemmed from his pride in me, his ambition for me.

Julio understood me even when I'd somewhat lost myself. The truth is that motherhood did not complete me. It was one substantial part of a much larger, and now neglected, whole. My love for my children and pride in their successes was important to me in a different way to the respect and admiration of colleagues and readers. Neither could compensate for the other. They did, however, enhance each other.

Becoming a mother put 'professional' life into perspective, moderating its ups and downs. Emotional inverted commas appeared around the 'tragedy' of a missed byline when framed against the backdrop of healthy, happy children; while a front-page byline made a child's whininess so much easier to tolerate.

And yet, Julio's words panicked me. After a year without deadlines and work-related travel I had lost confidence in the fragile, carefully scheduled world that I'd constructed for our family in Indonesia surviving without my constant, micromanaging presence. Mid-week trips to the paediatrician, parent–teacher meetings, sadistic school projects ('Next week is international week. Please send four different change of clothes representing major world cultures along with a few savoury and sweet dishes from your home country!) bopped anxiously in my head. How would I reconcile the infinite flow of demands like these with professional commitments?

I had become invested in the idea of my indispensability to the domestic. This was an inverted version of the malaise I occasionally accused Julio of: the idea that EU–Indonesia relations could not withstand his taking the occasional day off from work to handle an emergency at home. We all had a tendency to egotism. There was in fact little in the world that could not survive less of us, or be improved by a more balanced 'us'.

I hadn't imagined that I would ever come to see my primary responsibility as that of a housewife. The 'choice' to stay at home was not one I believed needed to be respected as much as to be defeated. 'Growing up' had tamed some of these views. The reality of the enormous amount of effort that running a home and caring for boisterous children takes had cut me down a few notches. The expat housewives I came to know in Jakarta were for the most part vibrant and hard-working, and did not conform to the ladies-who-lunch stereotype of frivolity.

Many of us could not work in Indonesia because of the difficulties foreigners have in obtaining work permits. Those with younger kids were usually too overwhelmed to consider professional lives. Others were unable to find jobs that were flexible enough to accommodate their needs. And some simply did not want to work outside the home.

But a further problem had to do with the loss of self-confidence that we experience after a few years away from the professional world. In the four or five years we stay at home shepherding children into grade school, technology moves on and skill sets change. The habits of discipline and focus that juggling work and life entail are denuded. It may usually be more rewarding to have both a public and private avatar, but it is unquestionably harder as well.

This is why Julio's admonishments filled me with unease. I'd only been away from reporting for a year or so, yet already my little grey cells felt oxidized. I could scarcely countenance the difficulties women on longer breaks had when attempting to re-enter the workforce.[5] My problems were negligible, if for no other reason than the happy fact that I had a job offer just waiting for me to sign on. All I needed was a kick up my backside, and Julio had stepped up to that task.

8

IDENTITY

2012–14, INDONESIA

I am an Indian who met a Spaniard in London and moved to China with him. We got married and spent the next decade living in Beijing, Brussels and Jakarta. The languages we share in common are English, Mandarin and some Bahasa Indonesia. Our Sunday family dinner ritual features sushi. Neither of us is religious but Julio reads the Gita, while it's fallen on me to explain to Ishaan (following a visit to the Prado art museum in Madrid) why the Romans were 'bad guys', apropos the crucifixion of Jesus Christ.

We are a tangy chutney of a family. We are spectrums: of skin colour, beliefs, identities. We reject ends that tie up. We want our souls to be capacious. We are greedy to embrace. We celebrate confusion. And yet, I worry.

In 2005, the year I married Julio, my father wrote a column for *The Times of India* titled 'My Family and Other Globalizers'. He talked about how both his children had foreign spouses. My brother lived in the United States with his German wife. My father explained that while readers might assume our family to have been born on a jet plane, in reality we were barely a generation or two out of an obscure village in south India called Kargudi.

My grandfather was one of six children, and so, two generations later, the size of the Kargudi extended family is over 200. Of these, only three still live in the village with the rest having moved across India and the whole world, from China to Arabia to Europe to America. This single family accounts for fifty US citizens today.

'Dismiss the mutterings of those who claim that globalization means westernization,' wrote my father. 'It looks more like Aiyarization, viewed from Kargudi.' But he clarified that Aiyarization did not mean global domination by Aiyars any more than globalization meant global domination by westerners. It meant instead, the acquisition of multiple identities.

'I am a Kargudi villager, a Tamilian, a Delhi-wallah, an Indian, a Washington Redskins fan, and a citizen of the world, all at the same time,' he said. 'When I see the Brihadeeswara Temple in Tanjore, my heart swells and I say to myself, "This is mine." I feel exactly the same way when I see the Church of Bom Jesus in Goa, or the Jewish synagogue in Cochin, or the Siddi Sayed mosque in Ahmedabad: these too are mine. I have strolled so often through the parks at Oxford University and along the canal in Washington DC, that they feel part of me. As my family multiplies and intermarries, I hope one day to look at the Sagrada Familia cathedral in Barcelona and Rhine river in Germany and think, "These too are mine."'[1]

The article hit a chord amongst the liberal intelligentsia in India and circulated on social media for years. I felt a frisson of pride every time someone forwarded it to my email inbox, sometimes without having realized that I was the daughter of the author. My father's Lenonesque imaginings encapsulated how I'd always conceived of identity, as something mutable and manifold, rather than unitary and fixed by place and birth. My parents had encouraged me to believe that who I was was not a fait accompli, but an active process of choice. And so choice had characterized my life to a far greater extent than that of most Indians. I read freely. I studied fleetingly. I smoked. I made many terrible choices and some good ones.

When I left India to read history at Oxford, I found that I didn't miss 'home'. The wonder of the new left me with scant time to feel the loss of the familiar. I was enthralled by the Hungarian, Brazilian and British friends I made, and didn't feel the need to seek out Indian ones. I discovered novel favourite foods: brie de meaux, sundried tomatoes, ciabattas and hummus. I developed strong feelings for Gloucestershire, which included reading the literary corpus of Laurie Lee, thanks to a Gloucester-born, musicologist boyfriend. I became a committed feminist, following passionate talks with my Italian-Canadian Rhodes-scholar housemate. My identity expanded like an inflating accordion.

Eventually, on my first day as a master's student at the London School of Economics I met Julio – a Spanish Sinologist, who rarely hung out with other Spaniards. He loved brie de meaux and hummus. He believed in gender equality. The stars were obviously aligned.

The geographically diverse life that Julio and I went on to build was thoroughly cosmopolitan, inhabited by the kind of 'global souls' that the writer Pico Iyer describes in his eponymous book.[2] Our friends changed countries of residence more often than most people change shoes. They spoke many languages. They were often hyphenated. They were always transitional.

When people asked us, as they often did, how we coped with our 'cultural differences', Julio and I exchanged bemused looks. 'It's true,' Julio often quipped, 'Indians are smelly and rarely take a bath, but I'm working on her.' On occasion I borrowed that line, replacing 'Indians' with 'Spaniards'. We pitied the narrow conception of culture the questioners had. We poked fun at their gaucheness. The query itself bounced off us. It didn't belong to our dimension.

Life zipped along quite happily with this munificence of multiplicity for a while. But then two bumps appeared on the road, more or less contemporaneously: the mid-thirties and children.

I felt the premonition that something was awry shortly after we moved to Indonesia. Increasingly the idea of socializing with expats began to leave me cold. Julio would return home laden with invitations from embassies around the world and I wasn't enthused by any. The time when it was exciting to meet a Norwegian qua Norwegian was long gone. Foreign-ness itself had become somewhat banal and tedious. I felt little patience for the mangling of my name into 'Plawi' or 'Palava' or any of the other iterations that was its cosmopolitan fate. I felt like I might scream if someone asked me about my caste. And I didn't really care if Indian food suited a random conversationalist's digestive system or not.

Instead, I spent more time on Facebook, smiling fondly over the antics of old school friends, looking at pictures of reunions that I could not be part of, and participating in conversations about Indian politics and policy. While planning a holiday to see the multicoloured volcanic lakes of Kelimutu in eastern Indonesia, I caught myself zoning out into a fantasy about eating kakori kebabs in Delhi's Khan Market – an old favourite haunt. Sometimes I felt an unfocused yearning that took me a while to recognize as nostalgia. My long dormant roots were twitching.

And even as I took to buying Bollywood movie CDs to play in the car, there came a day when Julio unexpectedly accused me of being 'lazy' in learning Spanish. We'd been together for a dozen years, he said. Surely I should be speaking Spanish by now. I gaped at him like a startled blowfish.

When we began dating in London I had curled up to Julio in a tender moment and asked where I could take Spanish classes. 'What for?' he'd replied dismissively. Julio had studied at a French school in Spain and lived in England since he was sixteen. He'd studied Japanese and Chinese at university. He claimed to dream in English. Spanish was not necessary for me to connect with him, he insisted. I should learn Chinese instead. Far more useful. And so I did. I moved to Beijing and learned Mandarin. That he was turning around and snapping at me for not speaking Spanish, after years of actively discouraging me to do so, was rather startling.

I had noticed a distinct tilt towards the old country in Julio's mental orientation over the last few years. It had begun while we were still in Brussels and the euro currency crisis destabilized the Spanish economy. This was a period when Spanish stocks collapsed, youth unemployment crossed 50 per cent and talk of Spain's exit from the eurozone filled the newspapers. The Iberian Peninsula's fiscal woes seemed to trigger Julio's latent nationalism.

Suddenly he began to insist we take all our holidays in Spain. If I mentioned a possible trip to Italy, he countered that Spain was more beautiful. If I suggested Greece, he claimed that Spain offered more variety. He bought me a pair of shoes because they were made in Spain. And he began to take an interest in Spanish soccer. I had always been amused, even a little proud, at how my 'Spanish' husband knew more about mah-jong than football. When I expressed surprise at his new-found passion for the beautiful game, Julio looked at me blankly. It wasn't 'new', he said. It was just something I hadn't known about him.

I suspect that it was something he hadn't known about himself. Or at least something he'd only just remembered. Life was like that. It revealed (and recalled) ourselves to us without haste, only in the fullness of time.

The signs were increasingly difficult to ignore. After years of conscious transnationalism, place and nation were laying their long-fingered claim on us. We were being reeled in by our heritage like hapless fish on a hook.

When I read Salman Rushdie's *Midnight's Children* as a teenager, there was a phrase on the first page of the book that had stuck in my mind. The protagonist Saleem says that he was 'handcuffed to history'. I used this expression during an interview for a scholarship to Oxford, when I was asked why I thought pursuing a degree in history to be important. Glib, of course, but the selection committee seemed to agree.

And as I inched past my mid-thirties towards middle age this truth was looming larger. I had gone to the same school from the age of five to seventeen. I'd had the same best friend from elementary through high school. I'd lived in the same neighbourhood for two decades. I'd eaten Indian food almost every day of my life until I was twenty. I'd known all my neighbours. I had a plethora of place-based markers with which to measure the passing of childhood and adolescence. Lodhi Gardens, Humayun's tomb, Connaught Place, Bengali Market, Khan Market – these were spaces that I had ownership over, a joint ownership shared with friends and others I didn't know, but who were nonetheless part of my tribe. I had a tribe. It was one that existed even if I ignored it.

For all the choices I had made about eating hummus and learning Chinese, there was a core to my identity that was shaped by the environment in which I had grown up, and that had little to do with volition. It was determined by repetitive cultural rituals and parental diktats: years of lighting diyas on Diwali and singing the national anthem in school assemblies; watching *Chitrahaar* on Wednesday evenings; learning Bharatanatyam twice a week;

eating chicken manchurian as a special treat; reading *Amar Chitra Katha* comics until I could use 'verily' in daily conversation.

Beneath all my globetrotting there was a nucleus of stasis. And for all that my identity was a work of bricolage, that nucleus anchored it. But what about when someone lacked this core? When they were without an anchor? When choice became an existential burden too heavy for them to heave around? When the pastiche of their constructed identity concealed a hollowness within? What about my children?

By the time Ishaan was six years old and Nico all of four, they had attended three schools involving language environments that ranged from French, to Chinese, to English. They did not have regular interactions with extended family. They did not know their neighbours. They had not imbibed the scents of cardamom and mustard seeds frying in hot oil from their mother's cooking: I did not cook. They'd never encountered a chicken manchurian. They were wholly undefined by place or nation.

The Chinese–English bilingual kindergarten the kids initially attended in Jakarta celebrated the diversity of its student body annually with a special assembly in which all the children were required to wear national outfits and introduce themselves in a 'my name is xxx, I am from xxx' format. Despite days of coaching by his teacher, Ishaan was resolute in his refusal to say he was 'from Spain and India'. Instead he insisted on being Chinese. 'I was born in China,' he explained. On the day itself he was browbeaten into mouthing the compromise formulation of 'I am Spanish, Indian *and* Chinese'.

By the time Ishaan was five he'd made his peace with the fact that he was not Chinese, but nonetheless he refused to embrace his maternal or paternal roots. 'You are Indian, mama,' he said. 'And Papa is Spanish. Not me. I am nothing.'

Nico appeared to accept his parental heritage but I suspect this was because he was more emotionally manipulative than his brother. It was my younger son's style to say things that elicited approval rather than reflected his true feelings on a matter. The fact was that if he ever spotted anything visibly Indian, the national flag, for example, or a woman wearing a sari, he would excitedly point it out to me by saying, 'Look, it's *your* Indian things.' I was Indian, and Nico and Ishaan were their own special category that didn't have a name.

'Mixed' marriages were almost more common amongst our circle of friends than those where the couple shared a common nationality. But the challenges of identity confronting our kids were particular given the peculiarly deracinated space that Julio and I inhabited.

I was incapable of passing down the same elemental sense of Indianness that my mother had instilled in me without my even having realized it. In part this was because the environments we lived in did not automatically reinforce aspects of Indian culture. But, in part it was me.

My Indian roots were very much underground. Cricket commentary did not provide the soundtrack to our home life. I almost never wore saris. We largely relied on cooks (Chinese, Brazilian, Indonesian), Julio and takeaway, for meals. The kids were consequently more familiar with *jiaozi* and baguettes than daal and roti. I remember the first time Ishaan was confronted with saag I'd tried to persuade him to try a spoonful by claiming that it was 'Indian guacamole'. Nico of the banana and raisin diet spent entire holidays in India refusing even a bite of Indian food.

I forced the boys into kurta pajamas once a year on Diwali, a festival that unfortunately tended to fall around the same time of year as Halloween. It was a no contest. No one in the children's peer group celebrated Diwali, but everyone loved Halloween. Every year the kids and I faced off over whether they should wear Batman outfits or Indian clothes for the festival. They seemed far more interested in making pumpkin lanterns than rangoli. They much preferred the idea of trick or treating to Laxmi puja. Every year I felt a little broken-hearted. But I had only myself to blame.

It wasn't as though Julio was doing a better job at transmitting Spanishness either. English was my first language, and English had been Julio's de facto first language for most of his life. He made occasional attempts to speak with the children in his mother tongue, but was not consistent in his efforts. He bought them books from Spain but ended up translating them into English when the children protested that they didn't understand.

We simply didn't seem capable of 'pure'. We were linguistic muggles. Nico's first word was in Chinese, *ge ge* or older brother. We used a random mix of Hindi and Spanish terms thrown into English sentences. Pajama drawstrings were always 'nada', rinsing the mouth after brushing one's teeth was 'kulla'. But we often used Spanish for body parts. Cheeks, especially before they were about to be kissed, were *mofletes.* As already noted, breasts were *tetas.* We used the Indonesian *macet* for traffic jam.

Our customary miscegenation of language and food hadn't merited much attention in our pre-parenthood lives. But now we began to notice it. The other couples we knew, even those where the mother and father were of different nationalities, seemed to be far better and more determined to pass down their cultural heritage.

Adding to the complexity of identity in our family was religion. I am a non-militant atheist. While I couldn't bring myself to believe in a divine being, I have little interest in discouraging others from faith. I realize how useful a strong belief could be for both individuals and communities when times were tough. And I like the rituals associated with religion, being privileged enough to pick and choose the parts of ritual that are colourful and reassuring rather than oppressive. And yet I am cognizant of the multiple brutalities practised in the name of religion and remain deeply suspicious of organized belief.

Julio was agnostic, less willing than I to admit to the absence of faith, yet uninterested in prayer or worship. A church was of greater interest to him for its architecture than as a house of God.

In Indonesia, religion is omnipresent. Although a Muslim-majority country, the state recognizes five other official religions. Belief in the divinity of the one God is part of the philosophy of *Pancasila* that forms the basis for the Indonesian constitution. All institutions from universities to beauty spas ask clients to list their religion on registration forms. The calls of muezzins punctuate the days. Festivals of many faiths from Easter to Vesak (Buddha Purnima) are marked as public holidays.

It is mandatory for schools to provide religious studies classes, although a 'moral studies' option can be chosen instead. This is what I picked for Ishaan and Nico. But on the first day of his moral studies class, Ishaan returned home agitated and demanded to know why I had not 'given' him a religion. 'Religion is complicated,' I answered, ad-libbing desperately. 'It's better to choose one when you are older.' 'But I am a Muslim,' said Ishaan. 'Didn't you know that?'

So, we had a Chinese Muslim on our hands with Ishaan, which while endearing was also worrying. How many years of therapy blaming his parents would Ishaan go through in the future?

I was delighted therefore when I discovered that in Jakarta it was possible to outsource the entire business of the acquisition of Indian 'culture'. A group of Indonesian Sindhis, most of whom had roots in the country stretching back to the immediate aftermath of the Partition of India, ran Saturday morning classes at a local temple where they introduced children to the main festivals of the Indian calendar. The kids coloured pictures of the Indian flag and learnt Sanskrit shlokas, did crafts activities that had them making jap malas and were bribed into attendance with chocolate masquerading as 'prasad'.

I lost no time in packing off both the boys to begin their journey into Indianness.

Within weeks my children had become incredibly pious. Every time Nico sensed he was about to get into trouble he took off for the drawing room and arranged himself in front of the bare-breasted bronze statue of the Goddess Saraswati that adorned our coffee table. 'Om,' he intoned with folded hands, one eye cocked to observe whether his religiosity was having an ameliorating effect on my temper.

Predictably with Ishaan, the classes unleashed a torrent of unanswerable questions. 'Where does God do poo poo? Is there a toilet in the clouds?' he asked chattily. On another occasion he pointed at the aforementioned statue of Saraswati in the drawing room and asked why God didn't wear underwear. Just as I was about to tiptoe out of his room at night, after having spent ages getting him to bed, he called out: 'If God made everything, who made God?' 'Why do you ask so many questions,' I groaned, not for the first or last time. 'Because God made me like this,' came the reply, pat. And we both dissolved into a long, happy giggle.

But piety was not always a laughing matter. Before long God began to be invoked to challenge my (already rather attenuated) authority. If I ordered the children to listen to me (eat your vegetables/ brush your teeth/ tidy up your toys), they would cleverly claim that God had issued contradictory instructions to them, which I needed to heed because God was my boss.

It only took a few months for Ishaan to ask the one question I had known was inevitable, but was nonetheless unprepared to address. 'Mama,' said Ishaan, frowning slightly one afternoon, 'God isn't real, right?' I opened my mouth to reply but nothing came out. 'Right?' Ishaan persisted. 'I don't know,' I answered eventually. 'Maybe She is.' But before I could feel proud of my nifty use of the feminine pronoun, I noticed how sad Ishaan looked. Suddenly I longed to reassure him, to affirm that there is a God, and a heaven where his grandfather was waiting watching over him. That the cosmos is designed by an omniscient force for good. That we are not chronically alone with our choices. But I said nothing.

Ishaan looked at me mournfully from under his long eyelashes. 'I don't think God is real,' he said. 'I just don't think so.' I hugged him tightly even as he wiggled to get away. 'I really don't know, darling,' I reiterated. 'It's something you will have to find out for yourself.' Nico came to the rescue at that moment by asking a question of his own. 'But can God defeat Darth Sidious?'

I would occasionally invoke God to enforce discipline, much in the way that you might tell your kids to behave so that Santa Claus didn't forget to bring them presents on Christmas. Occasionally, I'd make them pray to ask for forgiveness or assistance in resolving brotherly spats. I bought them tons of *Amar Chitra Katha* comics, illustrated books that I had devoured as a child myself, detailing the lives of an assortment of figures from Hindu mythology.

The kids loved them for all the gore, demons and cursing sages. I had forgotten how violent these stories were. But the damage was done. Even though I tried to lure them back to Julia Donaldson's anodyne rhymes, they were enthralled with Sugriva murdering his elder brother, the monkey king Vali. Nico decided he was the 'dark rakshasa' Mayavi, while Ishaan took on the persona of the ferocious demon Dundhubi.

In the meantime, in an effort to inject some Christian spirit into the house, Julio took to making up stories that featured a fire-and-brimstone-flavoured cast of characters named Jeremiah, Esther, David and Daniel. The Old Testament is so much more fun, he said, when I asked him why he hadn't opted for more turn-the-other-cheek narratives.

In a parallel development, Julio began to attend a Gita satsang that we had stumbled upon while looking for options for Indian culture classes for the boys. He became convinced about the utility of studying the Hindu scripture for investors and decided to write a book on the Gita for the stock market in Spanish.

In keeping with the spirit of the prevailing cultural confusion we switched the children to the Australian school at the beginning of our third year in Indonesia. The curriculum of the bilingual Chinese school they used to attend was increasingly being shaped by the fevered ambitions of Tiger Moms, and I was fed up with hours of homework following a school day that only gave out at 3 p.m. The other international schools were either too far from our home or closed for intake, which made the Australian school the only viable choice.

It was a lovely campus and Ishaan flourished, although his accent became even stranger and he developed a passing obsession with marsupials. A positive side effect from my point of view was his new-found interest in cricket. 'India is the best in cricket,' Ishaan took to telling his friends, a statement that may have lacked accuracy, but symbolized an engaging touch of hitherto wholly absent nationalism on his part.

Every Friday morning the school held an assembly at which the principal, a middle-aged Australian, handed out awards to students 'caught being good'. One four-year-old girl was feted for remembering to flush the toilet after using it. The contrast with the slapping ogre of my own schooldays could not have been greater. Merit certificates were also presented. Nico got his first one on his third week in school for 'consistently trying to put on his shoes and socks independently'. I doubt the Australians would recognize a Tiger Mom if one growled in their face.

As our time in Indonesia began its scheduled closing, my geographical angst kicked in anew. Where were we going next, everyone asked us – a query that seemed to deserve a reply suggesting an enthusiastic embrace of new pastures and exotic fauna. But all I wanted was to go home.

What a fraught word that had become. We had bought a house in Brussels. Was that home? Julio was going to apply for a job opening in Delhi, the city where my mother and many friends still lived. Was that home? We had even discussed a return to Beijing. Could China become home again?

When I was a decade younger and newly peripatetic, I used to jest that the home page of Google was the only 'home' I had or needed. But I had little patience for such repartee now that I had two kids, furniture in storage facilities around the world, my fortieth birthday zooming around, chronic insomnia and ageing parents.

I remember reading the British sociologist Anthony Giddens as a master's student at the London School of Economics. He'd written about globalization leading to a 'disembedding' of family and community as social interactions are lifted out of particular spatial–temporal contexts and reconstituted elsewhere.[3] I couldn't think of a better term to describe my family as we celebrated Halloween in Jakarta, danced to Bollywood music in Beijing, celebrated Chinese New Year in Madrid: disembedded.

But does all this post-embeddedness merely equal spoilt-brattedness on a global level? The political scientist David Miller describes 'cosmopolitans' as people who view 'the world as a kind of giant supermarket, where place of residence is to be decided by the particular basket of goods (jobs, amenities, climate, etc.) available there'.[4] This is what I worried about. Would my children grow up feckless, without any sense of real social obligations? Would their colourful global identities be doomed to an adolescent shallowness, lacking the profundity that more national, place-bound attachments engender?

What I wanted for my family was an identity rooted in a lack of bigotry and a commitment to epistemological pluralism, values that are free of place. My children will always carry the mongrel within them. I hope that makes them committed to the beauty of miscegenation, to be open to many ways of being: black and white and pink (as Ishaan describes his skin colour), Christian and Hindu and atheist, Chinese and Indonesian and Spanish.

Even as Julio and I had begun to feel the tug of our national identities as we approached forty, both of us were defined by values, experiences and beliefs that had nothing to do with being either Indian or Spanish. Our non-national identities were stronger than the cultural claims made on us by our respective places of birth. I had gained infinitely more than I had given up in living the life I had. I am Indian but also so much more than that.

I suppose your identity is the thing you never stop becoming. Much about Ishaan's and Nico's identity will continue to grow long after I cease to be the fulcrum of their lives. And much will be beyond my control to shape as a parent.

The path that my children are walking feels fragile and uncertain because it is new. And yet cosmopolitanism is old. In about 420 BC, the philosopher Democritus of Abdera wrote, 'To a wise man, the whole earth is open; for the native land of a good soul is the whole earth.'

The technologies that my boys are growing up with, the seamless crossing of space and time that they allow for, will also help them be less alone in their hybridity. There is no far away for them. I remember my father telling me about his weeks-long journey by sea to go to university in England in the 1960s. Once there he did not return home until the completion of his degree. Phone calls were too expensive to contemplate, so his only form of communication with family back in India was via letters. By the 1990s when I went up to Oxford, the journey was a ten-hour plane ride. I used cheap phone cards to call home every other week and email (albeit a clunky non-web-based version) allowed me to write to my mother almost every day. I flew back to Delhi for annual visits.

For my boys, Skype, WhatsApp and their ilk have slayed distance altogether. (When Ishaan was two years old he asked me what 's' stood for. 'Umm, the sun,' I'd answered distractedly. 'I don't think so,' he'd replied, as sassy as ever. 'I think "s" is for Skype.') They zoom across space both virtually and physically. They're used to the idea that travelling to Singapore from Jakarta can take less time than getting from one end to the other of the gridlocked Indonesian capital. Nico uses the word jetlag as a synonym for tired. 'I'm jetlagged,' he whispers sleepily, when he doesn't want to wake up in the morning for school.

The primacy of national identity is missing for them. But I remain undecided about how significant this absence is. Their loyalties and rituals transcend borders, but are no less powerful for it. They have affection for the peoples of all the countries they have lived in. They know several national anthems – although they are currently most familiar with the Australian and Indonesian ones. They are as used to women in headscarves as they are to ones in miniskirts. Their Sunday ritual includes a sushi dinner instead of rajma chawal, but is nonetheless part of the repetitive routines of childhood that nurture a sturdy sense of self. For my kids countries are merely lines drawn on a map. They are free of the overheated emotion of patriotism.

I can only try and make them aware of their enormous privilege, so that while they do not become defined by place, they remain grounded.

And set against my hopes is the fear of their confusion and possible anger at the trade-offs made on their behalf by the choices of their parents – a fear that they might turn to rigid certainties as a rejection of the ceaseless movement of their childhoods. Our family needs to be deep enough to allow their roots to hold firm. It's a big ask.

By the time I began writing this book life had developed a cyclic rhythm with upturns and downswings. I started to write for the newspaper and travelled to east Java to report on toilet entrepreneurs who had helped make their villages free from open defecation. In Flores I wrote about Komodo dragons and in Bandung I did a nostalgia piece on the Asia–Africa conference of 1955.

Julio continued to tread the path to middle-aged risk aversion. As I was about to take off on a Cessna aircraft to do a fly-past over the forests of Kalimantan decimated by palm oil plantation, he called me in a last-ditch attempt to dissuade me from boarding. 'You are a mother now,' he said. 'Are you sure you want to take these risks?' I did.

After about a year, I got sacked again when the newspaper decided to close the bulk of its foreign bureaus. I had nannies quit on me twice, always at crucial junctures just before I was due to travel on assignment. The children got stomach bugs or the flu every once in a while. They squabbled interspersed with declarations of eternal love. I worked hard at freelancing but made less and less money. Sometimes I slept better than normal, but the insomnia continued.

Yet there were many moments of grace, like the first time Ishaan read out a book for Nico, or when he made breakfast in bed for me. There was the time Nico announced that his 'brain was filled with love' for me.

As the boys grew older, Julio gradually became more involved with them. He played chess with Ishaan and took him for aikido classes. He spent ten days in Spain alone with the children while I attended a conference in New Delhi. He helped out more at bedtime. Nonetheless, I remained somewhat disappointed, and surprised, at the asymmetry between us when it came to caregiving. I continued to oscillate between convincing myself that I needed to accept the situation and refusing to do so.

On the one hand I realize that harbouring resentments is corrosive. It would do everyone some good, perhaps, if I make peace with the fact that the fifty-fifty parenting split I had envisaged was never going to materialize. On the other hand I am like a terrier on the issue of equality in emotional and temporal investment in child rearing. I simply cannot let it pass as 'normal' that I am the de facto diaper bag packer, nurse, secretary and coach for the kids, while Julio is the amiable and well-meaning, but often distracted, friend whose level of involvement in their lives depends on how interesting the political news of the day was.

I wish I could claim to have resolved this conundrum. But I can't, because I haven't. I continue to nudge (and sometimes push) Julio to do more. Sometimes I go on strike and refuse to send in Ishaan's lunch form on time in the hope that Julio will start doing it instead. But he doesn't, and it is me who gets the desperate call from school about Ishaan's missing food and it is me who ends up sorting it all out eventually.

Yet, as the years have passed, the intensity of feelings behind the battles with my husband, and with myself, have dulled. Sometimes I can almost glimpse a future where the kids will be off and I will be 'free' again. It evokes complicated emotions. We will all move forward, but there is no going back. Certain paths have been closed forever and there is a natural sadness at having grown up, at the nostalgia for the Me Who Was before I became a mother. But there is also a deep happiness in the Me Who Is and, therefore, a putative wistfulness for the loss that the kids growing up will entail.

It is easy to complain about motherhood. It is tedious and often thankless. It is exhausting and requires no small measure of abnegation. It is much harder to explain why motherhood is so precious. The joy is ineffable. Or perhaps it is simply the case that it is joyous rather than pleasurable.

In an essay, the British writer Zadie Smith demolishes the notion that joy is simply a more intense version of pleasure. Joy is in fact a very difficult emotion to manage, she says. Of her child she writes: 'Occasionally the child, too, is a pleasure, though mostly she is a joy, which means in fact she gives us not much pleasure at all, but rather that strange admixture of terror, pain, and delight that I have come to recognize as joy, and now must find some way to live with daily.'[5]

Joy, I too have discovered, is turgid with contradictions. It is painful happiness, a gain made deeper by loss.

9

THE BOOK

This is the most personal of the books I have written. It has scooped out large parts of my family's life for public consumption. It has required me to explicitly examine aspects of my marriage and my reaction to motherhood, shining a spotlight on emotions and experiences that are usually left unacknowledged, for good reason. The lack of scrutiny can protect us. One never knows what skeletons lie rotting in the dark corners of one's biography.

Julio, for one, was less than thrilled when I brought up the idea of this memoir. This is the first of my books that he has not read chapter by chapter in manuscript form. In fact he's refused to read it, period. He believes the entire work to be a long rant about his failings as a parent. I have tried to persuade him that he does not ultimately cut an unsympathetic figure. I've also made the point that it might actually help him to be a more equal parent were he to read my analysis with open curiosity. He might agree with it. I haven't managed to persuade him of either point.

I did, however, offer to give up on the project were he to so want. I had no right to write about matters that involved Julio and our children if he had serious objections. My husband frowned, but grumbled a reluctant acquiescence, 'Oh, write it, I suppose. If you must.' Unsatisfied with this grudging response, I demurred, declaring that I had decided not to go ahead with the book after all. 'No, darling, I won't write it if you are even a little uneasy. I'll email the publisher tomorrow and tell them the deal is off.' Julio was immediately anxious. 'But, you must,' he insisted. 'It's important to you. And it'll be a great book. Don't give it up.'

As I said, my husband is not an unsympathetic figure. He is, in fact, a hero. A flawed and forgetful hero perhaps, but one who pushes me to leap when I'm feeling fearful even to hop. (There are, of course, times when it is better to refuse to budge than to leap. We will therefore not be having a third child no matter how much 'leaping' in that direction my spouse encourages.)

As for the kids, they are ridiculously excited about being in a book. This is especially true of Ishaan, who imagines himself being written into the role of valiant protagonist. When I told him that the book is actually about how he has driven me mad, disabled my career and given me insomnia, he giggled uncontrollably. 'Noooo,' he gasped. 'That's so funny. Don't make me laugh so much.' Well, the joke will be on him when he's old enough to read it. I do feel a tad guilty when I imagine his future girlfriends reading the book, but the fact is that he has driven me batty (although he may well make the same charge against me).

Writing this book has been a high-wire balancing act. I needed to be honest, to risk vulnerability. Nothing wrecks a memoir more thoroughly than artifice. But as with all memoirs there were places I needed to draw a line in the sand. This book is not meant to hurt or expose my family gratuitously. And so while it tells the truth and nothing but the truth, it doesn't necessarily tell the whole truth. I doubt the 'whole truth' is containable between the covers of a book. The act of writing is selective by nature. And memory is especially choosy. To claim perfect recapture in a memoir is disingenuous. But the point of this book is not a blow-by-blow revelation of every incident, feeling or dilemma that motherhood has involved.

My decision to write it was spurred by the isolation and the shock I'd experienced when Ishaan made his debut. Childbirth might be a biological norm, yet there was little that had felt 'natural' about the experience, not physically, and certainly not psychologically. My body had felt violated; chewed up. Emotionally I'd been under extreme stress, compounded by the sleep deprivation. If anything, motherhood was an abrupt, violent upending of the normal.

And yet for thirty-three years, even as several aunties, and the occasional uncle, made solicitous inquiries about my child-bearing plans, no one had discussed with me how traumatic it could be: not my mother, not my peers, not my doctors and not the strangers on the bus who made happy faces and clucking sounds when they caught sight of my swelling belly.

Nor were there any wider societal messages that I might have picked up on through media representations, advertisements or the like. If anything, all the signals in the environment indicated the opposite: soft glowing. I find it truly astounding how parents, teachers, and society as a whole, conspire to set up mothers to fail. In India, at least, there is almost no tradition of motherhood memoirs. Parenting seminars are rare. There is less talk about preparing for the psychological and physical impact of motherhood in the public sphere than about black holes and, certainly, the price of onions. The idea, I suppose, is that if anything needs to be learnt, it will be transmitted within families from mother to mother.

Perhaps this is how it had once been, although I'm not sure that it was ever adequate. In twenty-first-century India it is glaringly insufficient. Economic liberalization has altered the material and social circumstances of the middle classes. Increasing numbers of people do not live with constant access to their mothers. Even those who have never left the borders of their countries of birth are living more disembedded lives. The medical and technological fields have marched into brave new worlds rendering much of what older members of families can teach, redundant or contradictory of the latest research.

Women have new and different expectations from their lives. Some of us are 'liberated', most of us remain subjugated to varying degrees, but all of us need to have a loud, public conversation about motherhood.

I wanted to write this book, in part, to break the interiority of birth and parenting. The separation between the domestic and public spheres is spurious. Keeping 'women's' concerns safely shuttered within the four walls of the home has served patriarchy well. But, if we are at all interested in gender justice, 'motherhood' needs to be dragged out of the home and into the public eye, so that it is seen, acknowledged and responded to by governments, employers and the wider public. This is not a conversation that only resonates in the West. And its relevance is not restricted to women. Writing a motherhood memoir is not some sappy, self-indulgent exercise. It is a deadly serious endeavour that risks personal exposure to illuminate aspects of universal issues that are usually and wrongly relegated to the periphery.

It was a difficult book for me to write not only because of the vulnerability it required but also because of the assumed frivolity of the topic. My previous books about China and Europe addressed matters of great power rivalry, wars, fiscal crises and high politics. The audiences at my book presentations are usually elderly men, often retired from the military or diplomatic service.

When I was asked about my next book the expectation was a work of reportage on Indonesia. And when I replied saying I was writing about motherhood, many even amongst my most loyal readers looked embarrassed. They didn't know where to place their eyes. Suddenly fidgety, their words imploded into mumbles and their smiles became forced. Over the last year and a half I've often been asked with barely disguised condescension, how my 'pregnancy book' is proceeding.

Nothing could have spurred me on to writing this book with greater passion than reactions of this kind. There is nothing embarrassing about babies or parenting. Motherhood is as, arguably more, important than war or border negotiations. It affects more people. Its socio-economic ramifications are immense. It is relevant to both genders and all nationalities. It is personal and political.

Rather than being uncomfortable and shifty when confronted with issues of parenthood, men need to be part of the conversation. Novelist Stephen Marche points out in an article in *The Atlantic* magazine that the absence of men from discussions of work–life balance is particularly strange given how 'decisions about who works and who takes care of the children, and who makes the money and how the money is spent, are not decided by women alone or by some vague and impersonal force called society'. They are in fact made by men *and* women with the central conflict of domestic life often not about mothers versus fathers, as much as family versus money.[1]

When I became a mother for the first time with Ishaan, the experience had sucker-punched me. I'd felt marooned on a new planet without a map. I wanted therefore to write the kind of book that I didn't have access to at the time, but would have clutched at raft-like had it been on my bookshelf. What I'd needed was something free of exhortations to breastfeed or sleep-train or rush back to work or bake cookies. I did not want an instruction manual. I did not want an ideology. But I would have liked to read a memoir that acknowledged the manifold ruptures that parenthood entails. A book that provoked questions rather than provided answers, so that I could start the important conversations I needed to have with doctors, parents, workplaces, my husband and myself.

The first publisher I approached with the idea for this book, however, was interested in an 'Amy Chua–like Tiger Mom' book for an Indian audience. Could I come up with something that tapped into cultural anxieties? Do the Chinese do parenting better than Indians? What about the Indonesians?

When I explained this was not the type of book I was about to write, the editor I was in conversation with zoomed into my interest on gender issues. How about my proclaiming that all women should work even after becoming mothers. 'Be bold,' I was urged. 'A book like this needs polemic.' (I was also told to avoid the word 'feminism' too much because it sounded 'dreary'.)

There certainly is an overflow of parenting books out there, although less in India than in many other parts of the world. No doubt, there is therefore a marketing imperative for a book on motherhood to distinguish itself with a 'strong, original argument', beyond the acknowledgement of complexity. 'Just make a statement in your opening paragraph. The complexity can come later,' an editor urged, when I pointed to the need for nuance.

It got me thinking about how many of the 'big' motherhood books are usually more subtle than their marketing slogans implied. Amy Chua's *Battle Hymn* is in part about the failure of Tiger Mom techniques. Sheryl Sandberg's book has been caricatured as an exhortation to women to work ever harder to serve the capitalist machine, when it is in fact a sensitive exploration of the myriad challenges faced by women in the workplace.

I mulled over the idea that perhaps it was worth succumbing to being marketed under a catchphrase, while publishing a more nuanced book by stealth. What would my 'strong statement' be? Attachment parenting is evil. Motherhood enslaves. You will hate your husband after you have children. Men must be forced to take paternity leave.

Some of these were conclusions I had toyed with. But they had as much to do with my own experiences, personality and circumstances as with Truth. They were hardly ready to be converted into 'isms' to hook potential readers into purchases.

I wanted to write an anti-theory book. Something that was about the compromises that women and men make and argue about; about imperfect feminism and the politics of the quotidian; about ideals meeting reality and reality being shaped by ideals; about the particular as much as the universal. I didn't want to write a 'categorical imperative' or a 'Platonic form'. I was neither Kant nor Plato. I was just a reporter and a mom, who had babies and bylines.

Broad-brush theories about parenting/motherhood continue to be consumed rather voraciously by women (and a minority of men) but they can be fatiguing and disappointing. This was certainly my experience as I ingested, often with pernicious (if hilarious) effect, a variety of parenting manuals. The world really didn't need me to join in on the preaching.

But I do have opinions and some advice. These may not resonate equally with everyone. The hetero-normative, materially privileged position I speak from imbues my views and priorities, although some of my 'takeaways' apply more broadly than others. Here are six of them. One for every year of Ishaan's life so far.

RESIST THE ALL-CONSUMING IDEOLOGY OF MOTHERHOOD

Every woman must find her own path across and through the variable geography of motherhood. There may be no single road, but every path should be walked without sacrificing the self-actualization of the traveller.

So many of the parenting theories bursting from the shelves of bookstores today are misogynist in effect, from the proselytizing of breastfeeding evangelists to the insidious idea that every little decision a mother takes – what to eat when pregnant, whether or not to sleep with the child in the same bed, and whether or not to put her kids down in front of the TV to get a break – will have deep, lasting effects on the child's character and behaviour.

One bit of 'research' claims that children who don't share their mother's bed until the age of three tend towards promiscuity in later life. According to a 2014 newspaper article in the UK's *Daily Mail*, titled 'Bad News for Dads: Babies should share mother's bed until age three because it's good for their hearts,' (Excuse me while I hyperventilate over the vile sexism of just the headline), if a mother does not have a baby sleep on top of her chest it 'makes it harder for mother and child to bond – and damages the development of the brain, leading to bad behaviour as the child grows up'.[2]

And then there is the Danish study that even made it to Indian newspapers, asserting that binge drinking by a woman *even once* during a pregnancy could cause the child to have a short attention span and be badly behaved. A drinking binge was defined as consuming two-and-a-half large glasses of wine.[3] The article quoted one of the researchers, Janni Niclasen of Copenhagen University, as saying, 'Women really shouldn't panic,' while warning that binge drinking early in pregnancy is known to raise the risk of miscarriages, stillbirths and birth defects. But don't panic, OK?

If living in so many parts of the world has taught me anything it is that 'science' is often a social construct. The answers to whether or not to get a massage when pregnant, or to have an epidural during labour, or to return to work when the children are still young vary dramatically depending on national and cultural contexts. What is considered safe in Belgium would appall most Chinese. And what the Belgians consider par for the course would horrify many Indians. In pregnancy and parenting, as in most aspects of life, risks are omnipresent. We cannot end risk. We can only make judgement calls, to the best of our ability, knowledge and needs. There is peace to be found in this truth. Especially for women. Drink some coffee, eat some spice. Choose what you are comfortable with, rather than allowing guilt to police your choices.

I also believe that a woman should prioritize herself at par with her baby. Too much sacrifice and abnegation is harmful to both the mother and her child. A woman is more capacious than a mother. She is not just a vessel. She is not just a caregiver. Her agency is powerful and deserves nurture, most of all by herself. The modern tendency to deify children and turn them into the sacred centre of marriages and women's lives is dangerous. We have gone from a society that had a pragmatic, somewhat utilitarian, view of children to one where children are worshipped. As sociologist Viviana Zelizer puts it, children have become 'economically worthless but emotionally priceless', morphing from useful to coddled.[4]

For those of us who are both liberated from the material need to exploit child labour, and uninterested in God, that is for the wealthy and secular, it is possible to argue that one's children are the new opiate. The effects of this shift on parenthood, but on motherhood in particular, can be regressive and oppressive. Not every woman needs to work, or work full-time, or to stay at home. But I do think that every woman needs to be defined beyond motherhood. What that means to an individual is subjective.

To me it means 'working' as conventionally defined: paid employment outside the home, although I am aware that this is because I am privileged by my education and upbringing to be able to perform work that I enjoy. Additionally, I believe that working moms are good role models for their children, both girls and boys. And here's some 'evidence' in support:

A May 2015 article in *The New York Times* detailed a new study of 50,000 adults in twenty-five countries that found the daughters of working mothers completed more years of education, were more likely to be employed and in supervisory roles, and earned higher incomes. The sons of working mothers spent more time on childcare and housework.[5] But the article also mentioned that according to a poll carried out by the Pew Centre, 41 per cent of adults in the US believed that an increase in working mothers was bad for society, while only 22 per cent said it was good.

Predictably there is also 'evidence' to prove that the disapproving 41 per cent majority are correct. A quick Google search turned up a study by the Institute for Social and Economic Research in the UK, according to which the children of mothers who return to work full-time in the years before they start school have slower emotional development and score less well in reading and maths tests.[6] Although the study did find that the consequences were less severe for the children of better-educated mothers, apparently 'even the children of highly educated mothers who go back to full-time work early, will have lower educational attainment'.

Ultimately there is very little evidence on the matters covered in this book that is incontrovertible. Rather, for every study there is inevitably a counter-study. Which is why one must rely on common sense. A happy mother will obviously have a better chance at ensuring a happy child. And it is a rare human being who can find happiness in sublimation, specially to a two-year-old tantrum-throwing brat.

PARENTHOOD IS THE TEST THAT MOST FEMINIST HUSBANDS FAIL

Julio is the perfect example of a modern and well-intentioned man, husband and father. In our pre-parenthood years, both before and after marriage, I was hard-pressed to sniff even a whiff of patriarchy about him. He cooked, I did not. He did not expect me to clean up after him. He appreciated my mind – an exciting thing. And he was not intimidated by my, ahem, forceful personality.

If the most critical career decision a woman can make is her choice of spouse, I had made an excellent one. Julio supported my career as though it were his own. He was patient with my fears, but helped me overcome them. He dreamed big for me and was never jealous of any success that came my way.

And yet once we became parents, gendered divisions reared up like bucking broncos running amok. Seven years into the parenting gig, Julio goes to office every day and is the financial mainstay of the home. I work part-time and earn the kind of pocket money that most writers, if they are lucky, manage. I fill out the children's lunch forms and make sure their snack bags are packed. I get their school uniforms ready every evening in preparation for the next day and make sure they wear matching socks. I know which child loves bananas and which one hates them. I've taught them to read. I force them to write. It's to me that they reveal nuggets of information about what's important to them. And it's I who usually puts them to bed.

Julio loves them dearly. He often makes them breakfast. He plays chess with Ishaan once in a while. He cuddles Nico a lot. He makes up stories to entertain them whenever he has the time. He's changed a few diapers in his time. He's attended a couple of parent–teacher meetings at school. But he does not do admin. He does not make to-do lists in his head before going to bed. He is so much less stressed.

Ultimately, even the most feminist of husbands often fail the equal parenting test because they assume less responsibility for the time-sensitive, human resource side of child rearing. It is mothers, working mothers included, who come under attack by what sociologists Annette Lareau and Elliot Weininger call 'pressure points', or non-negotiable demands that make lives feel more frenetic. The experience of these pressure points is not captured well in quantitative measures as in the amount of time objectively spent on a task. They represent rather a qualitative dimension of time use; how that time *feels*.[7]

The sense of near-constant urgency engendered by years of simultaneously supervising a three-year-old's bowel movements, brushing a six-year-old's teeth, arranging to interview the head of Indonesia's anti-corruption commission, and trying to remember whether Cake Stall day at school is this Friday or the next is summed up neatly in Jennifer Senior's book, *All Joy and No Fun: The Paradox of Modern Parenthood*, thus:

> Being compelled to divide and subdivide your time doesn't just compromise your productivity and lead to garden-variety discombobulation. It also creates a feeling of urgency – a sense that no matter how tranquil the moment, no matter how unpressured the circumstances, there's always a pot somewhere that's about to boil over.[8]

Julio and I might spend an equal number of hours looking after the kids (which we don't, but let us assume this for argument's sake); yet we will come out of the experience feeling very different. If he has an hour to spend with the kids he will read the newspaper and check the stock market on the iPad. His claim to babysitting will be that the children have been in the room with him. He will come out of the hour thinking about his stock portfolio and perhaps feeling a bit peckish.

I would spend the same sixty minutes questioning the children about their friends and activities, adjudicating their fights, reminding them to pack their items for their weekly 'show and tell' sessions, asking about missing water bottles and remembering to reschedule the older one's swimming class the following Tuesday because he'd accepted a birthday party invitation at the same time. I would come out of the hour with my nerves on edge and mind racing to accomplish all the tasks without forgetting any.

I am, like most mothers, the timekeeper, the maker of lists, the chief *reminder-er*.

A widely circulated May 2015 piece in *The New York Times* titled 'Mom: the Designated Worrier' points out that sociological studies of heterosexual couples from all strata of society confirm that mothers tend to draft the checklists while fathers pick and choose among the items.[9] Worse, 'worry work' can scatter a mother's focus and derail her career. The author, Judith Shulevitz, argues, 'This distracting grind of apprehension and organization may be one of the least movable obstacles to women's equality in the workplace.'

One reason women like me get stuck with the micromanagement of family life is that we don't see it coming at first. One day you're doing more of the admin because you're still on maternity leave while your husband has returned to work. You probably think this is perfectly reasonable. I did. But the next thing you know, you've been dumped with all the pulverizing minutiae of primary childcare, even though this was never your plan. As Shulevitz put it, 'She who buys the bootees will surely buy the bottle washer, just as she'll probably find the babysitter and pencil in the class trips.'

I don't mean to imply that women do everything for the kids. But most of them do a lot more of a certain type of task than their partners, even when those partners are 'feminists' in the sense of being supportive of their spouses' careers.

And it's not only the worrying about the nitty-gritty of family administration. As worriers-in-chief, women also manage to worry about the larger picture. I have spent what I'm sure would add up to years of my life worrying about not earning a high enough salary, about my children behaving inappropriately in public, about being too much of a disciplinarian, about not being strict enough, about my mother, about my father, about my mother-in-law, about the kids' future identity crises and mine. Phew! Did I mention that I don't sleep well?

The effects of parenthood on marriage were a surprise to me. From the days that Julio and I sat sipping wine and idly imagining a future family when we were still students in London, I'd assumed raising children to be something that would cement our bonds by underscoring our oneness of values. But I found that even the most well-intentioned, aware, and otherwise fair-minded couples could find their feminist principles undone by parenthood.

There is no easy solution to this unedifying state of affairs, which is why it persists with such remarkable stubbornness. The best one can do is to try and be prepared. Don't allow yourself to be lulled into a false sense of security. That way lies an ambush. Fathers need to be enlisted as joint human resource managers from the word go. The cartography of parenting is demarcated early on. Renegotiating the borders at a later date is harder than arriving at an equitable arrangement from the outset.

To this I'd also add the benefits of self-consciously deciding to feel at least 50 per cent less guilty about all things related to motherhood. This is an arbitrary number, but because it is concrete, it provides a tangible target. Cultivate the lack of guilt like a delicate orchid. And be tender with your flaws. There are few universal truths. That parenting is one long episode in making mistakes is one of them.

THE WORKPLACE IS MISOGYNISTIC

The modern workplace can be brutal for family life. If anything, the economic rewards of working longer hours are increasing. It is unsurprising therefore that men retain a significant edge in relative earnings, even as women today are better educated than ever before.[10] When overwork is rewarded and flexibility downplayed, women are automatically penalized.

Sheryl Sandberg shows how just the thought of the kind of hours high-profile jobs today entail puts many women off from trying for them, long before they are even pregnant. A kind of anticipatory self-sabotage.[11] And if it is women, rather than men, who will be taking leave once they have children and then require flexibility in working conditions while these children are young, it is perfectly logical for employers to favour men over women. The lack of a level playing field at work also inevitably perpetuates inequality at home.

All of which is why paid paternity leave is so important; not just the option of it but making it attractive, even mandatory. Nothing would normalize a more equitable role for fathers in childcare than strongly encouraged leave from work for new dads. The beneficial consequences for children, mothers and society in general would be significant. Several studies show children who have an involved father are likelier to be more emotionally secure, are better able to regulate their feelings and behaviour, and have stronger academic performance.[12]

If dads spend long hours being the primary caregivers for their babies, internalizing the idea that the buck stops with them (rather than exclusively with mothers), the importance of list making might just dawn on their newspaper-reading, football-watching, iPad-addled brains. I do not believe that men are by nature incapable of family administration. First of all there are already many stay-at-home fathers who are exceptions to the rule of mothers as coordination chiefs. Secondly, it's not as though many (most?) women *enjoy* domestic secretarial tasks. They do it because they don't have a choice. Normalizing paternity leave could change this perhaps.

It is also logical to assume that if dads do more at home, mothers would do better at 'work'. In Sweden, the country that has arguably done more to encourage paternity leave than any other, a study by the Swedish Institute of Labour Market Policy Evaluation showed that a mother's future earnings increased on an average 7 per cent for every month the father took leave. Daddy leave was first introduced in Sweden in 1995 to a lukewarm reception, but policy efforts over the next decade created a broad cultural shift. For example, from 2002 onwards, if the mother and father each took at least two months' leave, the family would get two extra months off. By 2006, 41 per cent of companies reported making a formal decision to encourage fathers to take parental leave, up from only 2 per cent in 1993.[13] And while in 1995, Swedish men took only 0.5 per cent of all paid parental leave, today they take a quarter of it.[14]

More paternity leave is not something that should be seen as an imposition on recalcitrant men under attack from militant feminists. Across the world, fathers are also chafing against the lengthening and increasingly unpredictable workday that has resulted from globalization and new technologies like the mobile Internet. The Pew Research Center released a study in 2013 showing that almost as many working fathers as mothers in the US said they'd like to stay home with their children, but had to work because they needed the income. Roughly the same number of fathers as mothers surveyed – about half of each – said that they had a hard time balancing work and family. Indeed, dads were more likely than moms to say that they wish they could spend more time with their children.[15] There have been similar findings in other parts of the world, including India and China.[16]

It is possible that, when confronted with the reality of the boredom and stress that looking after small children entails, many of these fathers who are ostensibly longing for greater time with their children, might change their minds. It is also possible that when they claim to want greater work–life balance what they really mean is less time at work and more time watching sports. Regardless, even the formal mouthing of a greater desire to be involved with the children is an important cultural shift, and can in turn encourage corporations to shift their policies.

On the day I wrote this section of the book the newspapers were full of the announcement that mothers *and* fathers who worked at Virgin Management, the Richard Branson Group's investment and brand-licensing arm, for four years or longer would receive 100 per cent of their salary for fifty-two weeks. There were geographical caveats that applied to this policy, but Virgin is only one of many companies that is gradually moving towards paternity leave, because many fathers and mothers are expressing a desire for it.[17]

The road ahead is long and pitted, but it's important for women and men to ask that employers recognize their needs as parents. This is not tantamount to demanding 'special' favours. Expecting to be able to live an existence where you can work and parent without fatally compromising one or the other is normal. It is the workplace's current practices that are pathological.

SCHOOLS ARE A LARGE PART OF THE PROBLEM

The sexism of schools is manifold. There is the literal sexism, which mirrors societal norms. A friend from Delhi, whose daughters attend one of the city's top schools, recalled in horror a nursery rhyme her children returned home singing one afternoon that went: '*Gaadi ka pahiya gol gol, papa ka paisa gol gol, mummy ki roti gol gol*' (the wheels of the car are round, papa's money is round, mummy's rotis are round). Parent–teacher meetings are often scheduled for times that exclude dads (and working parents in general).

But the biggest problem that schools present is that of school hours. These do not match the working day. Longer school hours and good-quality preschool day-care centres are not theoretical liberation. They would be tantamount to real freedom for women and men. It's been argued that childcare should probably be seen as something akin to utilities, a service like the water supply that any functioning economy needs in order to operate effectively and which benefits society, not just the individual user.[18] I agree.

It could be so simple: synchronize the school day with the workday. Poof! As if with the wave of a magic wand, so many of the travails of modern-day parents would vanish, just like that. And yet we remain far from achieving this as a reality, not only in 'traditional' societies where school norms are fundamentally shaped by assumptions about mothers staying at home, but even in so-called 'advanced' countries.

In Belgium, 66 per cent of mothers with children under the age of six work.[19] Yet, most schools close at noon on Wednesdays. How can this arbitrary practice not be considered misogynist? How many Belgian fathers are affected by half-day Wednesdays compared to Belgian mothers? I don't have the figures, but it would be a safe bet to guess the answer to be very few. If the modern workplace is at cross-purposes with feminism, so are schools.

Other than longer hours, there is much else that schools could do to help alleviate the specific burdens they create for mothers. They could plan parent–teacher meetings when most fathers are available to attend and specifically request their attendance. They could enlist fathers in organizing picnics or field trips and send them email requests regarding school projects. They could organize seminars on barriers faced by fathers in balancing work with family, so that 'balance' does not become something women must uniquely be responsible for.

And they could certainly start to use textbooks that not only depict strong female role models but also feature men doing some housework.[20]

THERE IS ONLY SO MUCH YOU CAN CONTROL ABOUT YOUR KIDS

I remember begging a five-year-old Ishaan with groggy-eyed frustration to try and sleep in a little later. 'You know, Mama, how some people are born blind?' he'd replied earnestly. 'Well, some people are born less sleepy.'

My kids are really not what I'd imagined them to be on the rare occasions that I'd indulged in such speculative fantasies in my pre-motherhood life. I'd imagined they would be girls. Also bookish and polite. I got boys who love *Stars Wars* and fight and fall and yell. They prefer football to books, and staging mock attacks on each other to fine motor activities.

It took me a while to realize, and even longer to accept, that ultimately kids are not robots that parents can programme and control, but their own people over whom parents only have limited control. This is a rather inconvenient truth because as a parent you are responsible for your children. Indeed you are *held* responsible for your children. And yet, there is only so much you can do.

People, including children, come in all flavours: friendly, grumpy, driven, lazy. You can try and instill kindness in your kids. And you can give them a wide range of opportunities, so that they can find and hone their strengths, while learning to deal with their weaknesses. And that's pretty much it. You cannot make them into concert pianists, whatever the Tiger Moms of the world might believe.

On the bright side, this truth should allow parents to cut themselves some slack. Accepting it reduces guilt – one of the biggest benefits possible for parents. Forcing a child to sit through endless piano lessons is no longer necessary. Use the time freed up to read a book instead.

HOW IT FEELS TO BE A PARENT AND HOW IT FEELS TO PARENT VERY DISTINCT

They can in fact be akin to antonyms: sublime and profane; rewarding and punishing; pleasurable and painful.

Jennifer Senior draws on the psychologist Daniel Kahneman's distinction between the 'experiencing self' that exists in the present moment and the 'remembering self' that constructs a life's narrative. 'Our experiencing selves tell researchers that we prefer doing the dishes – or napping, or shopping, or answering emails – to spending time with our kids. . . . But our remembering selves tell researchers that no one – and nothing – provides us with so much joy as our children,' she writes.[21]

This joy is what is summoned when we remember our lives' narrative arcs. The kind we feel when we gather around a kitchen table looking at old photographs, recalling first words spoken, or first days at school. It is the ineffable, profound, fuzzy high of family life rather than the energy-sapping torture of trying to persuade a toddler to put his dinner in his mouth, instead of on your clothes and carpets.

It is what underlies the tableaux of anecdotes that stay with you long after the irritations have evaporated. Like playing 'doctor-doctor' with a three-year-old Nico. I am the patient while he checks my throat and ears conscientiously and gives me some 'medicine'. But I'm not quite prepared when he lunges for my nether regions, solicitously stating, 'And here's some diaper cream for Mama.' Or the time when the boys cover me in a blanket, stick their teddy bears under my arm and switch off the lights in my bedroom. Then they close the door and exit arm in arm. 'We're the parents, Mama,' Ishaan says as a parting shot. 'You sleep tight.'

I feel pretty wrung out by the end of the day, on most days. But even minutes after the kids are in bed, if an old friend were to call to catch up, I'd probably tell them I'd never been happier – and mean it. As much as I have fantasized about running away in the middle of the night to become a pirate, or a janitor at a nice, quiet museum of modern art, or pretty much anything that does not involve taking care of young children and nagging an otherwise preoccupied spouse, I think my narrative arc, peopled as it is with Ishaan, Nico and Julio, is nigh on perfection.

Children push life off kilter. But it's a rare parent who doesn't eventually come to feel that their children helped them maintain equilibrium. In *Letters to a Young Poet,* the Austrian writer Rainer Maria Rilke wrote, 'We know little, but that we must trust in what is difficult is a certainty that will never abandon us.' Discussing this work in *The New Yorker*, Andrew Solomon points out that Rilke is not simply suggesting that we give up easier pleasures because those that are difficult are better, but that the difficulty itself is what makes those efforts so rewarding. Difficulty is not something just to be endured to get to a goal, but we must understand difficulty as part of the goal.[22] This is a profound truth that motherhood has driven home.

We are now in our last year in Indonesia and remain uncertain about where we will head next. But as Ishaan announced the other day, 'It doesn't really matter, Mama. Because they'll still have sushi there, right?'

NOTES

2. THE BABY

1. Even mothers in the middle ages seemed to need help. For women having trouble breastfeeding, forty-six pilgrimages to sanctuaries of Mary's Holy Breast Milk existed in France alone. ('Had the Virgin been a cow,' observed the sixteenth-century Protestant John Calvin, 'she scarcely could not have produced such a quantity.') See, Alain de Botton, *Financial Times*, 14 August 2015, *Why We Travel*, http://www.ft.com/intl/cms/s/2/f6653b82-4023-11e5-9abe-5b335da3a90e.html#slide0
2. See, Tara Parker Pope, 'Maternal Instinct Is Wired into the Brain', *The New York Times*, 7 March 2008, http://well.blogs.nytimes.com/2008/03/07/maternal-instinct-iswired-into-the-brain/?_php=true&_type=blogs&_r=0

3. SLEEP

1. Some studies have shown that women are hardwired to respond to crying babies. See, http://www.nih.gov/news/health/may2013/nichd-06 html National Institute of Health Study

4. CHOICE

1. 'The economic rewards of working longer hours have increased 236 over time, giving men a significant edge in relative earnings almost sufficient to countervail women's increased educational attainment and job experience—especially in professional and managerial jobs.'

– How culture of work and globalization are at cross purposes with feminism..., at http://www.thenation.com/blog/180031/doesfeminism-have-class-problem

2. 'Why the Mommy Wars rage on', http://www.more.com/reinvention-money/careers/why-mommy-wars-rage-0?page=2 Many surveys have shown that whether a respondent's mother worked while she was growing up has a strong influence on her own perceptions. Answers to who is a better mother, who is happier, who is a better role model depend not so much on the respondent's own employment status as on whether her mother held a job during her childhood. Respondents tended to think that what their mothers did was best, even if it wasn't the choice they were making for themselves.
3. https://www.youtube.com/watch?v=KtPv7IEhWRA
4. *Lean In* is the title of a popular book by Sheryl Sandberg, the COO of Facebook. The phrase 'leaning in' has come to be associated with the idea of women working harder to make it possible for them to enjoy both a career and family life.
5. There is a strong conviction amongst an elite demographic in the United States that everything in countries like France is better, including attitudes towards raising children. Bestselling books like Pamela Druckerman's, *Bringing up Bebe*, argue that by setting strict boundaries, refusing to indulge their children and insisting on focusing on their own needs as much as those of their offspring, French mothers ensure good behaviour and experience less stress.
6. http://www.mayoclinic.org/diseases-conditions/oppositionaldefiant-disorder/basics/symptoms/con-20024559
7. http://www.littleheartsbooks.com/2013/11/29/the-gift-of-a-strongwilled-child

5. RINSE AND REPEAT

1. http://www.theatlantic.com/features/archive/2014/04/theconfidence-gap/359815/
2. A number of studies have shown that women's pain is more likely to be dismissed by the medical profession as 'emotional' and 'psychogenic' than that reported by men. See, for example, Diane E. Hoffmann and

Anita J. Tarzian, 'The Girl Who Cried Pain: A Bias Against Women in the Treatment of Pain', *Journal of Law, Medicine & Ethics*, 29 (2001), 13–27, at http://www.forgrace.org/documents/hoffmann.pdf

3. The World Economic Forum's Global Gender Gap Report, 2014, found that the gap for economic participation and opportunity stands at 60 per cent worldwide, meaning that globally women had a mere 60 per cent parity with men on parameters of economic well-being, including a ratio of estimated female-to-male earned income. In contrast, the gender gap in terms of health and survival was a much better 96 per cent globally, with thirty-five countries having closed the gap entirely. At a relatively healthy 94 per cent globally, the educational attainment differential was also far narrower than that relating to economic opportunity.
4. Sheryl Sandberg, *Lean in: Women, Work, and the Will to Lead*, New York: Alfred A. Knopf, 2013.
5. Pamela Druckerman, *Bringing up Bebe: One American Mother Discovers the Wisdom of French Parenting*, New York: Penguin Books, 2012.

6. VALUE

1. 'Mothers put careers at risk with second child', *The Guardian*, http://www.theguardian.com/uk/2001/mar/18/bensummerskill.sarahryle A third child, unsurprisingly, makes matters even trickier. See, 'How many kids does it take to derail a career?', http://www.forbes.com/sites/meghancasserly/2011/07/14/how-many-kids-does-it-take-toderail-a-career/
2. Alice Walker, 'One Child of One's Own: A Meaningful Digression Within the Work(s)', *In Search of Our Mothers' Gardens: Womanist Prose*, San Diego: Harcourt Brace Jovanovich, 1983.
3. http://www.theatlantic.com/sexes/archive/2013/06/the-secretto-being-both-a-successful-writer-and-a-mother-have-just-onekid/276642/
4. Europe's already ageing workforce set to shrink by a million every year until 2050. See, Pallavi Aiyar, *Punjabi Parmesan*, New Delhi: Penguin, 2013.
5. See, Pallavi Aiyar, '*A Twist in Euro Tale*', *Business Standard*, 19 November 2011, http://www.business-standard.com/article/opinion/

pallavi-aiyar-twist-in-the-euro-tale-111111900067_1.html

6. See, Dayna Tortorici, 'More Smiles? More Money', *The Evil Issue,* No. 17, Fall 2013.
7. See, Georg Simmel and David Frisby (eds), *The Philosophy of Money,* London: Routledge Classics, 2011. See also, David Auerbach's discussion of the text on his blog: http://www.waggish.org/2014/georg-simmelsphilosophy-of-money/
8. Libby Anne, '*On Feminism and Embracing the Homemaker*', http://www.patheos.com/blogs/lovejoyfeminism/2014/09/on-feminismand-embracing-the-homemaker.html
9. See, Tom Hodgkinson, *The Idle Parent: Why Laid-Back Parents Raise Happier and Healthier Kids,* New York: Tarcher Books, 2010.

7. TOUCH

1. http://www.theatlantic.com/magazine/archive/2012/07/whywomen-still-cant-have-it-all/309020/
2. At the time of writing the teachers had been acquitted and serious doubts had also been raised about the veracity of the charges against the janitors.
3. However, much of parenting is hypocritical. We restrict screen time for children but sit in front of the computer all day ourselves. We don't let them drink sodas, even though we often drink a coke ourselves. Children and adults are not on a level playing field. And children instinctively grasp and accept this difference. The hypocrisy argument alone is therefore not sufficient justification against smacking as a disciplinary strategy.
4. http://www.telegraph.co.uk/news/health/news/10004517/Smacking-does-children-no-harm-if-they-feel-loved-study-claims.html. See also http://www.sciencedaily.com/releases/2013/04/130417114007.html
5. See, http://www.theguardian.com/lifeandstyle/2013/jun/16/can-women-stage-mumback-after-having-children. See also, http://www.telegraph.co.uk/women/mother-tongue/7051926/Returning-towork-What-mummy-did-next.html)

8. IDENTITY

1. Swaminathan Aiyar, 'My Family and Other Globalizers', *The Times of India,* 2 April 2005, http://articles.timesofindia.indiatimes.com/2005-04-02/all-that-matters/27836077_1_german-girlwedding-guests-bullock-cart
2. Pico Iyer, *Global Soul: Jet lag, Shopping Malls and the Search for Home,* New York: Alfred A. Knopf, 2000.
3. Anthony Giddens, *The Consequences of Modernity,* Cambridge: Cambridge, Polity Press, 1990.
4. David Miller, *On Nationality,* Oxford: Clarendon Press, 1995, p. 14. See also, Tom G. Palmer, 'Globalization, Cosmopolitanism and Personal Identity', in *Ethics & Politics,* 2003, 2.
5. *Zadie Smith,* 'Joy', *New York Review of Books,* 10 January 2013.

9. THE BOOK

1. http://www.theatlantic.com/magazine/archive/2013/07/themasculine-mystique/309401/?utm_source=SFFB
2. http://www.dailymail.co.uk/health/article-2054393/Bad-news-dads-Babies-share-mothers-bed-age-good-hearts.html
3. http://www.business-standard.com/article/news-ians/drinking-during-pregnancy-could-lead-to-badlybehavedkid-114012500704_1.html
4. Viviana A. Zelizer, *Pricing the Priceless Child: The Changing Social Value of Children,* New Jersey: Princeton University Press, 1994.
5. http://www.nytimes.com/2015/05/17/upshot/mounting-evidenceof-some-advantages-for-children-of-working-mothers.html?_r=1&abt=0002&abg=0
6. http://www.theguardian.com/money/2003/nov/14/workandcareers
7. 'Time, Work, and Family Life: Reconceptualizing Gendered Time Patterns Through the Case of Children's Organized Activities', *Sociological Forum,* Vol. 23, No. 3, September 2008.
8. Jennifer Senior, *All Joy and No Fun: The Paradox of Modern Parenthood,* New York: Ecco, 2014. See also, *Why Mom's time is different from Dad's time,* http://www.wsj.com/articles/SB10001424052702304757004579335053525792432
9. 'Mom: The Designated Worrier', *NYT,* 8 May 2015, http://www.nytimes.

com/2015/05/10/opinion/sunday/judith-shulevitz-momthe-designated-worrier.html

10. 'The Global Gender Gap 2014', World Economic Forum: http://www.weforum.org/reports/global-gender-gap-report-2014
11. Sheryl Sandberg, *Lean in: Women, Work, and the Will to Lead*, New York: Alfred A. Knopf, 2013.
12. www.childwelfare.gov/pubs/usermanuals/fatherhood/fatherhood.pdf, http://www.livescience.com/37435-fathers-importance-kids.html 'The role of fathers in children's lives: A view from urban India', http://www.freepatentsonline.com/article/Childhood-Education/250133777.html
13. http://www.nytimes.com/2010/06/10/world/europe/10iht-sweden.html?_r=0.
14. 'Why Swedish men take so much paternity leave', *The Economist*:, 1 July 2014, www.economist.com/blogs/economist-explains/2014/07/economist-explains-15
15. http://www.pewsocialtrends.org/files/2013/03/FINAL_modern_parenthood_03-2013. See also :http://www.theguardian.com/lifeandstyle/2010/nov/04/fathers-happier-morehousework-study
16. 'Work-Life Balance: A Challenge for Both Genders in Asia', *Wall Street Journal*, 17 May 2012, http://blogs.wsj.com/indiarealtime/2012/05/17/work-life-balance-a-challenge-for-bothgenders-in-asia/
17. http://time.com/3916636/virgin-paternity-leave/
18. Andie Fox, 'The difference between working dads and working mums', http://www.dailylife.com.au/life-and-love/work-and-money/the-difference-between-working-dads-andworking-mums-20140812-3dkh4.html
19. http://www.statisticbrain.com/working-mother-statistics/
20. Less than four per cent of the biographical figures in French history books are women. See http://www.worldcrunch.com/ culture-society/france-s-sexist-school-textbooks-only-11-womenhistory-makers/c3s4166/#.VXv0dqaprL9. See also, Deepti Pria Mehrotra, 'Sexism and Patriarchy in the Textbooks: Good girls are submissive and subsidiary', http://sacw.net/article3339.html
21. Jennifer Senior, *All Joy and No Fun: The Paradox of Modern Parenthood*, New York: Ecco, 2014.
22. http://www.newyorker.com/books/page-turner/the-middle-ofthings-advice-for-young-writers?mbid=social_facebook

ACKNOWLEDGEMENTS

I am grateful to my village of readers and fellow mums in Jakarta, Delhi, Beijing, Boston, Washington, DC, Baton Rouge and Canberra. Huge thanks: Ira Singh Tharakan, Maria Jose Palleres, Smita Maitra, Suranya Aiyar, Tuva Kahrs, Manjari Chatterji Miller and Franziska Ohnsorge. Particular thanks to my namesake Pallavi Rastogi for editing like the English professor she is. *Merci beaucoup* to Rebecca Fabrizi for her close (and quick) reading and response.

Shukriya to Karthika, who is the sharpest and loveliest of editors, as well as the entire team at HarperCollins India, especially Bidisha, Amrita and Bonita. It feels good to be 'home' with them.

Gracias to Kiran Ganguli for his gentleness, and for the seminal role he played in my childhood. It is not only parents who parent us.

Much gratefulness, for everything, to my mother, Gitanjali: superior wielder of poky-poky, gentle-gentle and Nani nonpareil.

A deep thanks to my father, Swami, for embracing the world and for helping me to do the same. And *dankeschön* also to my brother, Shekhar, for being the dad (and sibling) he is.

I owe bucketfuls of *xie xies* to Julio for his unflagging encouragement, as well as his permission to write about us. I am happy that he eventually read the bulk of the manuscript, despite his irritating tendency to skip ahead to the bits about himself.

This book is dedicated to my precious brats, Ishaan and Nicolas, the two most interesting and infuriating people I know. May they forgive their mother her manifold flaws.

And *terimah kasih* to all the dads who read this book. Much hope resides in you.